AF490103

SMART QUIT®

CASH IN. CLOCK OUT.

SMART QUIT®

CASH IN. CLOCK OUT.

DREA LYNN

© 2026 by Andrea Holmes. All rights reserved.

No part of this publication may be reproduced, distributed, or transmitted in any form or by any means, including photocopying, recording, scanning, or other electronic or mechanical methods, without prior written permission of the publisher, except in the case of brief quotations used in reviews, articles, and other critical commentary.

For permission requests, contact:
Drea Lynn Publishing
info@drealynn.co
ISBN: 979-8-9946828-7-6

First Edition.

Scripture quotations referenced in this book are taken from GOD'S WORD® Translation. GOD'S WORD® is a copyrighted work of God's Word to the Nations Mission Society. Used by permission. All rights reserved.

This book reflects the author's personal experiences, research, and perspective. It is not intended to provide legal, financial, medical, or professional advice. Readers should consult with qualified professionals before making decisions related to career, finances, or business.

Publisher: Drea Lynn Publishing
Cover Design: Drealynn.co
Interior Design: Drealynn.co

Dear God, thank you for walking with me through this entire journey and placing Smart Quit on my heart. I am continuously humbled by your grace and faithfulness.

Mom and Dad, thank you for every sacrifice you made to ensure I had the foundation I needed to succeed.

Peter, David, Miriam, and Gabrielle, thank you for reminding me that I am loved, supported, and seen, no matter what.

Randi, thank you for being the voice that says "keep going" when giving up feels easier. You have been my safe place in the moments I needed strength that wasn't mine.

Shea, true Black Girl Magic. Two out of 800, and you made sure I was never alone. This journey would have ended early without you. Forever grateful.

And to every boss, client, colleague, partner, and customer, thank you! Your lessons, support, challenges, and collaboration are the reason Smart Quit exists and your influence is woven into every page.

MORE
RESOURCES

CONTENTS

PHASE ONE
PREPARE

PHASE TWO
POSITION

PHASE THREE
PIVOT

PHASE FOUR
PROFIT

EPILOGUE

Fortune favors the bold.
Latin proverb

THE EMAIL CAME IN LIKE ANY OTHER.

Subject: Department Sync (Conference Room B)

Nothing urgent. Nothing dramatic. I didn't think twice.

I was used to it. I was the one they called when things needed to get done and needed to get done right. My calendar already looked like a game of Jenga. Every block imperfectly balanced. Every move carefully placed, but one shift away from collapse.

Meetings stacked on meetings. Decisions. Deliverables. Expectations. People counting on me more than they'd ever actually know.

This was my normal.
But that day… something felt different. Not in the room, but in me.

I took my usual seat. Everyone settled in. Someone cleared their throat. And then came the updates. The kind that say everything and nothing at the same time:

Restructuring… Alignment…. New priorities…. Leadership shifts.

I was fine. More than fine. Safe. Trusted. Needed.
They needed me. They always did.
And for a long time, that felt like my purpose.
That day, something broke in me.

Not because I didn't care. Not because I wasn't grateful. Not because I didn't love the people I worked with. It was because I realized something I had never allowed myself before to admit. I was building systems, solutions, and success stories for everyone, but myself.

I was the one they relied on. The fixer. The go-to. The one who could take chaos and turn it into clarity.

The queen on the chessboard. Moving everywhere. Covering every gap. Holding everything together.

I was powerful but the power wasn't mine. I was leading, but I was not setting the destination. I was growing but not into who I wanted to be.

And some truths once seen, cannot be unseen.

I tried to push it down. I tried to "be grateful." I told myself I was just tired and that the moment would pass. It didn't.

Because the truth was this:
I wasn't exhausted from the work.
I was exhausted from abandoning myself inside the work.

I smiled through the rest of the meeting. I nodded. I contributed. I carried it all, like I always did. But I knew my time was up.

Not because the company no longer served me, but because my purpose was growing louder than my comfort.

What I didn't know was how to leave without burning my life down. How to step into my purpose without losing my stability. How to quit without it being a catastrophe. I would learn it the hard way.

That's why this book exists. So your story doesn't have to start in exhaustion, fear, or a six-figure freefall.

You don't have to leap blindly. You can be strategic and intentional. You can protect your peace, your finances, and your identity. You can leave well and launch well.

You can Smart Quit.

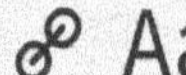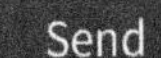

**Don't wait until you're in crisis to build your strategy.
Prepare in peace so you don't panic in pressure.**
Phil McGraw

INTRODUCTION

From a six-figure salary to six figures in debt. That's where my entrepreneurial story began. Not in triumph. Not in freedom, but in struggle and confusion. It became a very expensive lesson in what happens when you leap without a plan. That journey is what led me to write Smart Quit.

Thankfully, a few chapters into my story, the tide turned. I built a consulting business from zero to nearly half a million dollars in revenue in a little under three years. However, I'll be honest with you, it didn't have to take as long as it did, and it didn't have to hurt as much. If I had applied the tools, frameworks, and mindset shifts I share in this book, I could have avoided unnecessary stress, financial strain, and self-doubt.

My hope is that you and the entrepreneur within you, can learn from my lessons and strategically position yourself to transition smoothly from your paycheck to your purpose. This is your roadmap to build your dream without burning your life down in the process.

This book is not about bashing companies, corporate leaders, or the 9-to-5. In fact, it's quite the opposite. This is a celebration of the workplace, the modern training ground where the next CEOs, founders, and leaders are being shaped every day. Your job is not the enemy and it's not what's stopping you or holding you back. Your job is the resource you already have: real-world reps in strategy, leadership, discipline, communication, and solving the exact problems you'll face as a business owner. That is entrepreneurial gold.

For many of us, the workplace has replaced or extended the university. There is far more to learn about launching, scaling, and leading a successful business from inside a business that's already thriving, than from case studies in a textbook.

You are not wrong to work for someone else. You are being strategic. Now it's time to flip the script and use what you're earning and learning to fund what's next.

Entrepreneurship is the great equalizer that levels the playing field. It doesn't care who you are or where you came from, it only cares where you're willing to go.

Unlike traditional career paths that often require specific degrees, years of experience or even the right connections, entrepreneurship doesn't care if you are twenty-one or fifty-five, have an MBA or are a high school dropout, or if you are pivoting from a corporate career or flipping burgers at a fast food restaurant. You have a shot and there is a successful entrepreneur that started where you are today.

Your job is not the enemy.
Your job is your investor.

It will fund your dream, develop your discipline, and sharpen your skillset.

How to Know If This Book Is For You

If you're questioning whether the entrepreneur in you is real, ask yourself which of these sounds like you:

The Burnt-Out High Performer
You're great at your job; top tier, recognized, rewarded, promoted. Yet inside, you feel detached, drained, and done. Successful on paper, empty in reality.

The Under-Challenged Dreamer
Your role is "fine", but too easy. Too predictable. You're coasting and you know you're built for more.

The Company Loyalist
You've been with your company for years. You once thought you'd retire there. But now… the culture is shifting, leadership is changing, the ground feels shaky, and something in you is waking up.

The Side-Hustler
You have a full-time job, but your excitement lives in your passion project. Your mind is already working in two companies, however only one is paying you for it.

The Entrepreneur in Hiding
You have an idea. A calling. A vision. But your fear has been louder than your purpose… until now.

You don't have to relate to all entrepreneurs, but if you see even a glimmer of an entrepreneur in yourself, that's all the proof you need. You have what it takes.

You do not have to stay stuck.
You do not have to burn out.
And you definitely do not have to choose between stability and purpose.
There is a smart way to exit.

You may become rich working for someone else. However, no one becomes wealthy by only cashing a paycheck. You can build wealth, freedom, and legacy, but it requires ownership.

There are over 359 million companies worldwide, with over 3.6 billion workers. There is a point in every person's career cycle where they realize they were built for more. Being an employee creates income; being an owner creates legacies. This is the foundation of Smart Quit.

A quote attributed to Ralph Waldo Emerson says "The hand cannot create anything higher than the heart can imagine." We already know your destination: Living on purpose. Creating impact. Building legacy. Smart Quit is your how. A strategic, intentional, and disciplined transition.

This is your opportunity to take your leap and give yourself the best chance to land on solid operational ground when launching your new business. Smart Quit is your guide on how to Prepare, Position and Pivot yourself so you can successfully Profit in your new business.

Entrepreneurship doesn't care about your resume, it cares about your resilience and resolve. No matter your background or bank balance the pathway to success is open to you. The key is making smart, strategic decisions as you move forward with clarity and confidence.

This book won't tell you to quit your job today or storm out of the office waving your middle finger. That's the opposite of smart! This is about making your exit your greatest asset. We're talking about financial preparation, emotional readiness, strategic timing, skill stacking, and mindset rewiring.

This is not a rebellion. It's a revolution...with receipts.

So, let your Smart Quit begin.

Stage One: PREPARE

It always seems impossible until it is done.
Nelson Mandela

CHAPTER ONE
HERE ARE THE FACTS

Growing up, I was taught that work was about survival, stability, responsibility, and not disappointing others. Both of my parents were hard workers and instilled those values and a high level of discipline in me and my four siblings.

Do the right thing. Be grateful. Do your best. Earn your place. Don't make waves. Work hard. Stay loyal. Advance slowly. If you get a good job, keep and protect it.

For a long time, those beliefs made sense. Honestly, they served me well. They're what helped me become successful and pursue excellence in everything I do. Disciplined. Reliable. Trusted. A person people count on.

Here's the truth most people don't realize until it's too late. The same beliefs that help you rise can be the same beliefs that keep you stuck. Not because they are wrong, but because they were never designed to take you where you're going next.

We were taught to optimize for:
Safety instead of purpose

Approval instead of alignment
Job security instead of ownership
Not disappointing others, while abandoning ourselves

There's a feeling that arises when the spirit wants more, when it becomes clear that the current environment no longer fits. It may not feel exciting at first. It can even feel confusing or uncomfortable, like betrayal. There may be a sense of guilt, as though something is being done wrong. That's not the truth. It is simply the recognition that the old rules no longer apply to your evolved self. Patterns, expectations, and routines that once worked now feel limiting. What was once sufficient is no longer enough.

Before diving into strategy, transition plans, business building, visibility, or income shifts, it's essential to unlearn myths that no longer serve you and uncover the truths that do.

MYTH #1: Freedom automatically comes with entrepreneurship.

Entrepreneurship rarely begins with freedom. In the early stages, entrepreneurs are often consumed during long mornings, late nights, and weekends by the work itself. The role of an early owner demands wearing every hat: CEO, marketer, bookkeeper, customer service representative, sometimes even janitor. Every decision falls on one person, often without guidance, mentorship, or a clear roadmap. Income is unstable, swinging between periods of feast and famine. Even when revenue grows, such as reaching half a million dollars in your third year, you can still struggle with profitability, and personal celebration may never arrive.

The mental load is heavy. Self-doubt and impostor syndrome can dominate, particularly when comparing progress to your peers and competitors. Loneliness can creep in, pressure is high, fear of failure looms, and sometimes fear of success emerges as well. Entrepreneurs fund their businesses with personal savings or credit, navigating unexpected expenses and late-paying clients. Tax obligations, legal compliance, and operational responsibilities fall entirely on the owner.

Investments must often precede readiness: marketing campaigns, coaching, technology, tools, and staffing. Mistakes in hiring are expensive lessons. Training and managing a team while simultaneously executing core work is draining. Letting go of control is difficult, and trust in others to represent the brand requires intentional cultivation. Technology will fail; systems break; automation glitches. Work-life boundaries blur. Social events, family time, and personal priorities are often sacrificed. Profits may be reinvested repeatedly, delaying any reward of success. There are no guarantees. Everything depends on the decisions, discipline, and vision of the one running the business.

Even with these challenges, entrepreneurship, when approached strategically, can be more fulfilling than remaining in a role that will never align with your aspirations. It offers the opportunity to build a legacy, to create wealth, future freedom, and influence that extends beyond personal labor.

MYTH #2: Employment guarantees financial security.

Employment can feel safe, but it is often more uncertain than it appears. Organizations change, restructure, merge, or downsize, and there is little control over these shifts. A boss leaving or being replaced can drastically alter visibility, opportunities, and career trajectory. Projects relied upon can be cut. Budgets may tighten, leaving even high performers vulnerable to layoffs. At-will employment, common in many states, means termination can occur with minimal notice, often with limited or no severance.

Time and output belong to the employer. Earning stops when work stops. Raises are incremental; promotions are rare and often tied to politics rather than merit. Bonus structures fluctuate year to year, frequently influenced by decisions outside of individual control. Retirement plans, 401(k) matching, or pensions are uncertain or underfunded. Stability, while perceived, is an illusion, and the reliance on external decision-makers limits long-term wealth-building and autonomy.

Though entrepreneurship does not promise immediate freedom or overnight success, it does, offer sovereignty. It provides the ability to set direction, design systems, and create independent revenue streams. In a world where even "secure" jobs carry hidden risks, creating something of one's own can provide the most reliable form of stability.

TRUTH #1: The first and greatest investor is the self.

Your time, energy, skills, and talent are already being invested daily. Redirecting a portion of that investment toward building a future beyond the walls of your current employment is a strategic move. Every decision, meeting, task, or project can become a step toward freedom. Skills learned, networks built, and experiences gained in your current role serve as capital for entrepreneurial growth. Strategic employment transforms each day into intentional progress toward independence, rather than passive consumption of time.

TRUTH #2: Your employer is already an investor too.

Salary, benefits, access, and exposure provide resources to fund your entrepreneurial ventures. Current employment can act as a seed funder for future growth: paying for courses, software, early prototypes, virtual assistants, and other foundational tools. Decisions regarding your current role should be guided by objectivity, gratitude, and strategy rather than resentment or frustration. Detachment from ego, status, and title ensures that actions support long-term goals.

Entrepreneurship can begin while employment continues. Every paycheck, every benefit, and every opportunity can accelerate this transition. Knowledge, networks, and stability accrued in your current role provide leverage for the next chapter. Resources are wasted only if left unused. Strategic utilization allows momentum to build, while preserving energy, credibility, and professional relationships.

Suffering, resentment, or burned bridges is unnecessary. Employment can be leveraged as capital to fund a vision. Momentum is created through strategy and intentional action, not struggle. Every resource, skill, and connection from the current role can become fuel for freedom. Decisions become deliberate steps, and actions align with the long-term vision.

Purposeful transitions ensure that work contributes to wealth, freedom, and legacy. Career shifts become bridges, not leaps, into uncertainty. Foundations laid in your present role support sustainable growth, long-term success, and the ability to create a life that extends beyond limitations.

Stepping into entrepreneurship isn't about burning bridges or leaving everything behind. It's about being intentional with the life and future you want to create. Every choice you make now, every skill you build, every connection you nurture, and every dollar you save can become the fuel for your next chapter. Your current job isn't the enemy. It's your investor, giving you resources, experience, and stability while you lay the foundation for your future.

The real power comes from taking ownership of your path. You don't have to wait for permission, perfect timing, or the "right moment" to start building the life you want. Small, consistent steps matter more than big, dramatic leaps. Each step you take while still employed moves you closer to independence, freedom, and the kind of business that can grow without depending on your every hour.

Remember, this isn't just about making money. It's about building wealth, freedom, and legacy. You are creating something that lasts beyond you, that you control, and that can support not only your dreams but your peace, energy, and life. Every day you stay intentional, every choice you make with your future in mind, is a step toward your Smart Quit. This is the moment when you leave on your own terms and step fully into the life you've been building all along.

Real People. Real Quits. Real Wins.

Steve Wozinak

Smart Quit Age: 25 years old (co-founded Apple in 1976)
Education: B.S. in Electrical Engineering and Computer Science (completed his education later after Apple's founding)
Economic Background: Middle-class upbringing; father was an engineer, mom was a homemaker.

Steve Wozniak is widely recognized as one of the most influential engineers in history as the co-founder of Apple with Steve Jobs. However, prior to Apple, Wozniak worked full-time at Hewlett-Packard (HP) earning a modest salary. He had access to HP's world-class engineering environment, tools and spare electronic components. With these resources HP became Apple's first investor, without Wozniak breaking the rules.

Wozniak used HP's engineering tools and labs to prototype the Apple I after hours, he spent nights and weekends designing and coding the Apple I in his free time. He bootstrapped Apple I's entire product development without the need of investors by holding down his full-time job.

Apple I was originally offered to HP, and rejected FIVE TIMES, but Wozniak continued to believe in himself, invest in himself and took the leap of faith. Though not wealthy, he personally funded Apple by selling his beloved HP-65 calculator to raise funds for Apple's launch (Steve Jobs sold his Volkswagen van) becoming Apple's initial investor. This covered the initial startup costs to buy parts for the first batch of Apple I computers.

HP was not Wozniak's enemy. The company was an integral part of Apple's future success. It was an indirect investor in Apple's launch and Wozniak used his relationships, skills, tools and resources to kickstart his entrepreneurial journey.

Most of us are familiar with the rest of the story. Apple created some of the world's most iconic products, including the iPhone, iPad, MacBook,

Apple Watch, and AirPods - each redefining its category. Since launching the iPhone, Apple has sold over 2.3 billion units and generated more than $1 trillion in iPhone revenue alone. With a market valuation consistently with over $2 trillion, Apple remains one of the most profitable companies in history, earning almost more than $400 billion in annual revenue.

Steve Wozniak used his job at HP, not just for income, but as a springboard into his entrepreneurial future.

**The chains of habit are too light to be felt
until they are too heavy to be broken.**
Warren Buffet

CHAPTER TWO
GROUNDHOG DAY

It wasn't a dramatic breaking point. No slammed door. No meltdown. No single conversation that changes everything. One day, you just walk into a meeting you've walked into a hundred times before… and you know things have changed. Not with the room or your coworkers or your boss, but with you.

For me, it was the day I pulled into the parking lot, parking in my normal parking space. I left the ignition running and looked at the clock on the dash, 7:55 AM. The time seemed to taunt me because I knew I only had minutes before I was expected to walk into the doors leading to my office. I felt paralyzed, unable to move.

What happened to the days where I jumped out of the car, excited about the challenges and the new experiences my work day would bring? Today, as I finally moved to turn off the engine and open the car door, I felt like there was a five pound weight hanging on to each motion..

"Let me just get this day over with," I said to myself. In that moment, I realized this wasn't the first time I had felt this way, but I was finally allowing myself to acknowledge it. More importantly, it was the day I decided something had to change.

The building was the same. The people were the same. The projects were the same. I was not. I still showed up, still contributed because that's who I was. But something had shifted. Maybe you can relate.

There was a subtle internal voice whispering, "I cannot do this anymore." What should I do? I tried to work my way out of it. I figured if I gave more effort, more commitment, more clarity, or more patience, it will fix it. It did not. It wasn't about effort. It was about my identity. It had shifted

I wasn't just tired. I had outgrown a version of myself, and I realized I was built for more. That evolution followed a predictable emotional pattern.

This pattern is a loop. A cycle that most go through multiple times before they ever have the awareness and courage to leave it. I call it, The Stuck Cycle.

The Five Stages of The Stuck Cycle

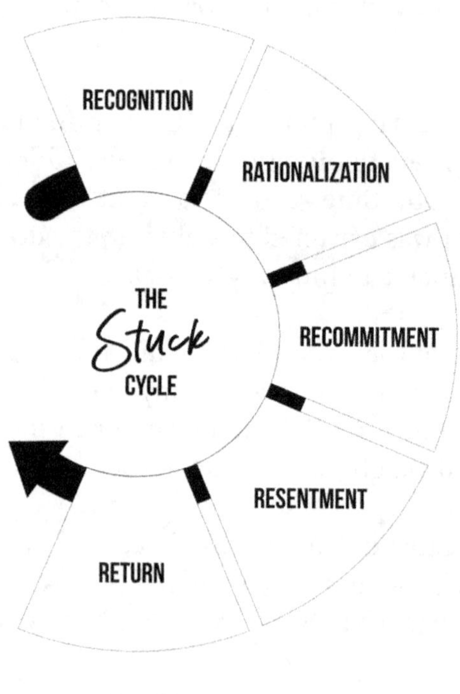

Stage One: Recognition
An internal shift is noticed. Something awakens.

Stage Two: Rationalization
The shift is explained away. "Maybe it's just stress." "Maybe a vacation is needed." "Maybe the problem is me."

Stage Three: Recommitment
Effort doubles. More hours. More responsibility. Trying to bring an "old feeling" back

Stage Four: Resentment
Effort fails to restore alignment. Feeling undervalued, unseen, or unfulfilled rises, even when everything looks fine on paper.

Stage Five: Return
The cycle brings a return to the starting point-but not as the same person. Return is wiser, more aware, and less willing to pretend. Eventually, the discomfort of staying outweighs the fear of leaving.

Real change begins not when a resignation letter is handed in, but when waiting for permission ends.

Breaking down each stage of the cycle helps identify where the mind and body are signaling misalignment and clarifies what the next move could be. We are gaining a better understanding of evolution, not focused on rushing an exit. Once the stage is named, drifting can end and a new direction begin.

No busywork.
No worksheets.
Just honesty.

WHERE IN YOUR JOB ARE YOU PRETENDING TO BE "FINE" WHEN YOU'RE ACTUALLY NOT?

Say it to yourself,
even if only in a whisper.

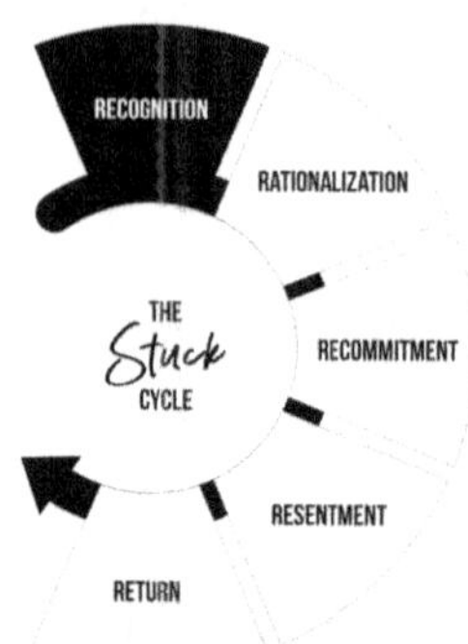

Recognition
(aka: "This isn't a phase.)

A shift doesn't happen overnight. Signs often appear long before awareness sets in:

A deep sigh before logging on.
Sunday-night tension.
The quiet question: "Why continue this?"
Excitement seeming to exist elsewhere.

Recognition occurs when the truth already known is finally acknowledged. Current circumstances no longer fit. Nothing is necessarily failing yet because tasks are still be completed. However, the role once aligned now feels limiting because growth has expanded beyond your old container. Your spirit has evolved, capacity increased, and identity shifted.

A position that once felt right, now shows its constraints. This is not from reaction or frustration, but as a reflection of authentic, mature growth. There is movement toward someone bigger, deeper, more intentional, and more rooted. Discomfort comes not from being lost, but from emerging into a new version of oneself.

Recognition marks awareness that: "The person who chose this role is no longer the one in it." Therefore, decisions must change accordingly.

This awareness doesn't wait for public signals, LinkedIn updates, or new business ventures. It begins with admitting: "Remaining here is no longer an option because potential exceeds current boundaries."

No permission, proof, or perfect plan is required at the start. Facts are faced,

Say this out loud
Yes, actually out loud:

I AM ALLOWED TO WANT MORE. AND I DON'T NEED A CRISIS TO JUSTIFY IT.

Let it land.

feelings acknowledged, fears observed. Recognition is not the exit, it is just the starting point of truth.

The power begins here.

Rationalization
(aka: "Maybe this is just me being dramatic…")

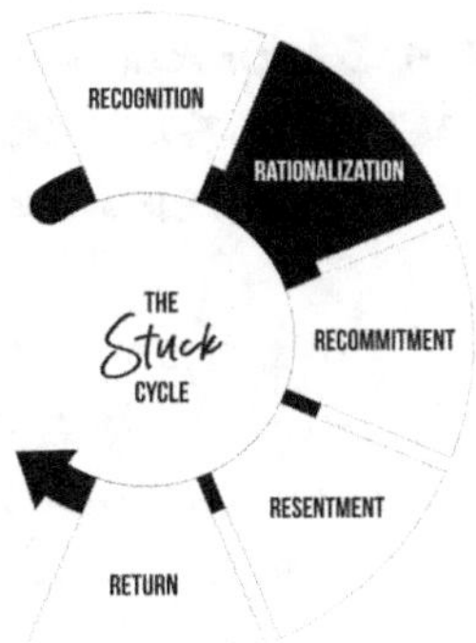

Once the shift is recognized, the mind immediately tries to talk itself out of it. Your brain's priority is not your fulfillment, it's survival. Thriving requires more than survival. Resistance surfaces to keep the familiar in place and ignoring it is like negotiating with a hostage negotiator inside your head.

The inner conversation might sound like:

> "It's just a rough week."
> "I'm just tired."
> "This is normal."
> "Others would be happy with this role."
> "I'm being ungrateful."
> "I just need to stay positive."
> "Maybe after this next project / quarter / reorg / fiscal year / leadership change / solar eclipse… things will feel better."

No. It will not.

If stress alone were the issue, rest would fix it. Breaks have been taken, PTO used, yet the truth always returns. This isn't fatigue, it's misalignment. Misalignment does not heal with time off.

Here's the hard part most avoid, rationalizing exists because facing the consequences of clarity is scary. Recognizing that a current role has run its course forces the decision about what comes next.

Terrifying? Absolutely.

Ask yourself
no filters, no performance:

AM I WORKING WITH MY FULL SELF OR THE VERSION OF ME THAT LEARNED HOW TO SURVIVE?

If the answer is anything other than whole, you should already know what comes next.

Not because of weakness, but because the next chapter demands ownership, clarity, and trust in self. These skills often unpracticed.

Here's the upside, rationalization signals awakening. It's not regression, it's resistance and resistance always precedes growth. If the mind is in overdrive insisting, "everything is fine," take note, your evolution is underway.

Movement has begun.

Recommitment
(aka: "I'll try one more time…")

Now comes the double-down phase, not out of belief in the work, but out of fear of what leaving would demand. This is the "try harder" stage, right before resentment sets in.

RECOGNITION

RATIONALIZATION

THE *Stuck* CYCLE

RECOMMITMENT

RESENTMENT

RETURN

Effort increases, hours stretch, responsibility grows. The instinct is to lean in, focus, and carry the weight because quitting is not an option, right? Thoughts sound like:

"If I just show up differently…"

"If I give it one more quarter…"

"I haven't tried everything yet…"

"I just need to prove something…"

Energy pours into a space already full. At first, it seems effective. Productivity returns, rhythm appears restored. Others notice. Praise may arrive and performance may look normal. However, inside everything is drying up. This is self-abandonment disguised as dedication.

The kicker? It works... temporarily. "See? I can handle it. I just needed focus," becomes the mantra.

Answer this with honesty:

WHERE ARE YOU CURRENTLY SHRINKING TO MAKE OTHER PEOPLE COMFORTABLE?

Say it plainly.
No justifying.
No softening.

Truth is your first step out.

Then cracks appear. Laughter fades. Excitement dulls. Creativity shrinks. Patience thins. Joy drifts away. Work still gets done, yet your presence is absent. Subtle at first, unnoticed by others, but unmistakable to the one living in it. The difference between giving your best effort and giving what remains grows impossible to ignore.

Recommitment feels noble, responsible, maybe even honorable. It's the "mature" choice. Yet no amount of effort can overwrite the disconnection. Passion does not return through grit alone. This phase signals the quiet start of resentment, a warning that the current path is no longer serving growth.

Resentment

Resentment is the heavy cost of staying in a role that no longer fits. At this stage, most people won't notice what's happening because everything continues to appear normal on the surface. Work still gets done, deadlines are met, and reliability remains. On paper, everything seems fine, but inside, everything has shifted.

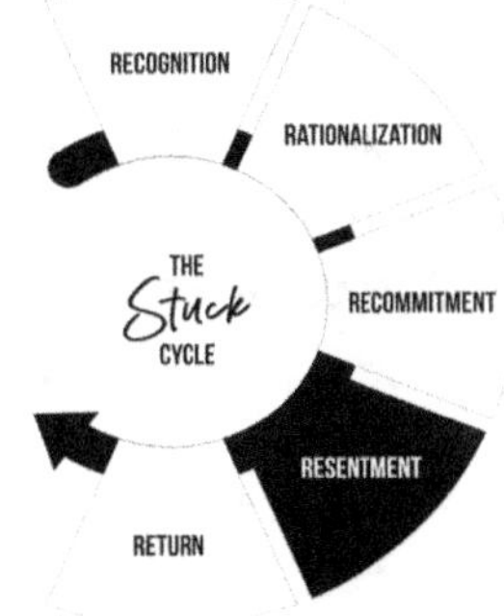

Resentment isn't loud. It's not anger toward a boss, the company, or the work itself. It is slow self-betrayal, a quiet erosion of satisfaction. It sounds like:

"Why am I still here?"
"Why am I pretending I don't know what I want?"
"Why am I holding back?"
"Why am I choosing comfort over calling?"

The ache comes from knowing there is more capacity than is being expressed and watching the potential remain untapped. The frustration is not aimed at the position, it's all internal. Your heart knows:

Smarter decisions are possible.
Greater gifts remain unused.
True calling is waiting.
Preparation is already in place.

The reality is undeniable, even when uncomfortable. Fulfillment is missing because your role has been significantly outgrown. Fear intensifies, whispering, "What if failure comes?" Life feels pulled in two directions: purpose urges expansion, fear pressures stagnation. That tension is exhausting.

Burnout emerges. The tasks aren't heavier, but it is exhausting pretending to fit. Energy fades from working below potential. Resentment signals the threshold has been reached. Though sometimes mistaken for ingratitude, impulsivity, or entitlement, resentment is not any of these. Even if surroundings remain unchanged, these are indications that your identity has evolved.

Complete this sentence:

IF I KEEP REPEATING THIS CYCLE, I KNOW IT WILL COST ME

____

Don't look away from your answer.

That's Truth calling your name.

Stage Four proves a vital truth: resentment is not failure. It is data. It marks the point where an exit is necessary. So what follows when that exit is embraced?

Return
(aka "I Have a Choice...")

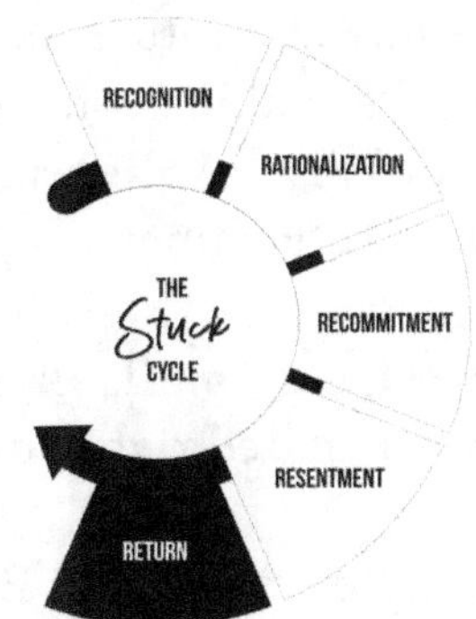

Most people don't leave the Stuck Cycle the first time it ends, or the second, or even the third. Many return to the beginning simply because familiarity feels safe. Staying also postpones hard decisions a little longer. What happens next? The loop restarts again.

Over and over. Quarter after quarter. Year after year. Until something finally shifts. The longer the cycle repeats, the more energy and confidence shrink to fit it. Creativity dulls, courage is delayed, and disconnection from purpose grows.

At this point, two paths appear: remain in the familiar, comfortable, and predictable, or finally break the loop. Staying may feel responsible or stable, but it slowly erodes vitality. Escaping the cycle requires facing the truth.

Name the Truth
Examine what truly isn't working. Document it without sugarcoating. Track the emotional, mental, and physical costs of staying stagnant.

Key Question: If nothing changed in the next six months, how would life really feel?

Disarm the Excuses
Identify the stories being told in your mind. Feelings aren't facts; facts are facts. Feelings often reflect fear, not reality. Examine each excuse logically. Are these concerns grounded in truth, or just fear-based beliefs? Fear of change doesn't signal unreadiness; it signals being human.

Key Questions: What's the worst-case scenario of leaving? What if the outcome is better than expected?

Shift the Energy
Instead of recommitting to the stuck cycle, recommit to your values, goals, health, and future. Let Smart Quit guide your next steps. Start building networks, making connection calls, and defining financial milestones. Momentum kills fear. Repeat: *momentum kills fear.* Small steps chip away at emotional attachment to your current role.

Key Question: If advising a close friend in this situation, what action would be suggested right now?

Use Resentment as Fuel, Not Cement
Notice resentment without burying it. It signals needs and values being ignored, even if self-imposed. Instead of letting frustration harden into bitterness, channel it to energize your exit strategy, your Smart Quit.

Key Question: How can this resentment become a starter for real change?

Commit to the Exit Strategy (Non-Negotiable)
Once the decision is made, set a clear timeline and define milestones. Secure accountability through a coach, mentor, or trusted friend to prevent backsliding. Create an emotional anchor; a vision board, a list of reasons, or a note for challenging days.

Key Mantra: "Growth over comfort."

True freedom starts when the script flips: the job is no longer a trap but a training ground. Every skill built, every relationship nurtured, every opportunity seized becomes part of an entrepreneurial toolkit. Entering the "unstuck cycle" means stopping the spin and steering toward a new future.

Your current role isn't an obstacle. It's a launchpad to prepare, position, and propel you into the life and business that truly matter. The only barrier between stuck and unstuck is the choice to see the present differently and act with purpose.

What once felt like grit quietly became the Stuck Cycle, repeating effort without forward motion and mistaking endurance for progress. Recognizing the shift opens space for a smarter move. This isn't giving up. It's quitting smart. Smart quitting is not failure, but discernment. We are closing a chapter honestly, taking the lesson without carrying the weight, and redirecting energy toward growth. The ending isn't an escape. It's a reset.

Growth is deliberate. Not "quit tomorrow," not burning it all down, not reacting from frustration or panic. Growth is stepping into a version capable of leading in your next chapter. Shrinking to fit a room already outgrown ends today. Stop negotiating with your calling and don't wait for your circumstances to force action.

As a Smart Quitter, growth is intentional, measured, strategic, and grounded. Clarity about goals comes with building the skills and systems to support the next level. As an owner you will move differently because you thinking has shifted.

"I am preparing for the life I am stepping into."

Smart Quitting blends courage with alignment and purpose isn't optional. Your Smart Quit is not a hobby or a side project. Your purpose is the assignment and growth is how it's answered.

So we're not beginning with the resignation emails, business launches, or public declarations. We are starting with how to stop the self-betrayal and how to replace apathy with clarity: "I am not going back to sleep on myself." The Return is not the exit. The Return is reclamation.

Forward motion starts now moving from knowing to owning, wishing to choosing, and feeling called to answering the call. No need to move too fast, or recklessly, but methodically and strategically. Staying? Already outgrown. The question now is "How can my exit become the start of something bigger?"

That is your Smart Quit.

Real People. Real Quits. Real Wins.

Michelle Obama

Smart Quit Age: ~27 years old (left Sidley & Austin law firm in 1991)
Education: B.A. in Sociology, J.D.,
Economic Background: Middle-class upbringing; father a city pump operator, mother a homemaker and secretary

In her memoir *Becoming*, Michelle Obama talks very candidly about working at the prestigious law firm Sidley Austin and realizing early on that it wasn't what she wanted to do with her life.

She had checked all the boxes; Ivy League degrees, a great salary, a high-profile job - but something felt off. She went through the motions, often questioning, "Is this all there is?" But even with that discomfort, she stayed because leaving felt like failure, or like throwing away all the work she had done to get there. She started rationalizing if her "off" feeling was wrong because she would be a failure or would have wasted her time and all she had done if she left.

However, eventually, she made the leap and entered into public service and community engagement, which was her dream. Even then, she knew she had stayed too long because she feared disappointing others or "wasting" her law degree which made her stall. Looking back, she realized that fear had ultimately costed her a lot of joy.

After becoming the first African American First Lady of the United States, Michelle Obama used her platform to champion education, health, and military families, launching impactful initiatives like Let's Move! and Reach Higher. After the White House, she became a bestselling author, global speaker and podcast host on leadership and empowerment. Her success was built on authenticity, service, and a relentless commitment to lifting others as she climbed.

32

Change your thoughts, change your life.
Tony Robbins

CHAPTER THREE
EMPLOYEE TO CEO

The moment was quiet, but it finally hit: I had been operating with CEO-level capacity in a role that only recognized me at as an employee-level contributor. Leading, solving, anticipating. Building systems and carrying responsibilities that often went unnoticed. I was the go-to person when things needed to get done, and done right. This was not because of a job description, but because it was core to my way of working.

Here's the disconnect: applying CEO-level capability to fulfill employee-level expectations and execute someone else's vision creates friction that cannot be ignored. Not boredom, not burnout, not confusion but an identity misalignment. Many have outgrown roles that they still perform. When identity evolves, the environment eventually must follow.

Most people make the same mistake. Work cannot transform without changing the way of being and thinking. In addition, a business cannot be led by a boss who is thinking like an employee. It will never work. Employees wait to be chosen, seek permission, perform to be evaluated, succeed by meeting expectations. CEOs claim themselves, take responsibility, create opportunities, and succeed by setting direction. This is not about titles. It's ownership of their time, value, decisions, and purpose.

Smart Quitting never starts with a resignation. Thinking about what comes next only at the moment of leaving is already too late. Preparation, positioning, and capitalization must come first, long before the last day at an employer is known.

Smart Quitting begins the moment life stops being outsourced. There's no need to become someone new, only to reclaim full ownership of your time, choices, and purpose.

The Before-and-After Identity Shift

Reevaluate:

    How you think

    How you lead

    How you decide

    How you value your time

    How you value your voice

    How you take up space

When an identity shift occurs, there is no going back. At this point, quitting becomes real. You are committed to forward movement and regression is no longer an option.

Say this out loud because your voice matters here:
"I am not waiting to be chosen. I choose myself."
Let it land.

This shift is required to strategically rewire how decisions are made, changing your internal operating system entirely. Until now, your internal wiring has been shaped in Employee Mode.

In Employee Mode, value is measured by how well someone else's plan is executed, how consistently expectations are met, and how reliable, efficient, and low-risk, performance appears. Always in service of someone else. Success in Employee Mode is defined by following direction, minimizing mistakes, and staying dependable.

That can make someone excellent at the job, and chronically stuck.

However, in CEO Mode, value is measured by one's ability to set direction, clarify vision, own decisions and lead through influence. Delivery alone is no longer enough. A CEO sees patterns, anticipates needs, creates opportunities, takes calculated risks, and leads rather than reacts.

An internal identity shift is choosing to take back control of your life for yourself.

5 Shifts from Employee to CEO Mode

Permission to Ownership
Stop asking, "Is this okay?" Start asking, "Is this aligned?" Employees wait to be chosen. CEOs choose themselves.

Task Execution to Vision Setting
Stop measuring value by productivity. Start measuring by direction. Ask daily, "Where am I leading myself?" not just, "What did I get done?"

Avoiding Mistakes to Making Decisions
Employees try not to get it wrong. CEOs focus on moving forward. The question isn't, "What if the move is wrong?" It's, "What happens if no move is made at all?"

Being Needed to Being Effective
Identity gets tied to being the reliable one, the fixer, and always dependable. These are the things that got you this far, but it won't take you where you need to go. Effectiveness isn't carrying more; it's choosing impact over overwork.

Proving to Owning

Capability doesn't need proving. You've done that for years. The real question now is will your talent and skills be applied to the future being built, or keep building someone else's?

Stop waiting. Start moving.

Beware: If you exit your current job in Employee Mode, you will build your business overworking, undervaluing yourself, underpricing your expertise and waiting for someone to validate you. When you leave in CEO Mode, you will build with clarity, confidence, authority, direction and ownership.

This employee to CEO shift will be revisited in Part 3, of Smart Quit, Pivot. Here, just remember, the difference is not skills. The difference is identity. Ask yourself, "Where in my life am I waiting for someone else to choose me, when it's my job to choose myself?" Clarity lives in your answer. New identity will determine your direction.

Now that your identity has shifted, we can now define the future you are building toward. Not vibes. Not dreams. The playbook.

Real People. Real Quits. Real Wins.

Mark Cuban

Smart Quit Age: 25 years old (left his sales job in 1984 to start MicroSolutions)
Education: B.S. in Management
Economic Background: Middle-class upbringing in Pittsburgh; father was an automobile upholsterer, mother held various jobs

Mark Cuban wasn't born wealthy. He grew up in a working-class family in Pittsburgh. After college, he moved to Dallas and worked various jobs, including bartending and selling software. He was fired from a sales job at a software company for closing a deal instead of opening the store on time, an early sign of his entrepreneurial instincts.

In 1983, he started his own company, MicroSolutions, a computer consulting business. He had no money and lived with six roommates in a small apartment, often struggling to pay bills. He lived frugally, sometimes skipping meals, using expired discount coupons, and driving a beat-up car. At one point, he was nearing an empty bank account, maxing out credit cards and surviving paycheck to paycheck.

Cuban kept learning and grinding. MicroSolutions eventually gained traction, and in 1990, he sold it to CompuServe for $6 million. His first big win.

Years later, he co-founded Broadcast.com, an internet radio streaming service. In 1999, during the dot-com boom, he sold Broadcast.com to Yahoo for $5.7 billion in stock, catapulting him into billionaire status.

Being broke did not mean that Mark was broken. He remained resourceful and hungry. He always invested in himself, not just financially, but by constantly learning about tech and business. He was resilient and turned setbacks, like getting fired, into opportunities. His frugality, focus and forward thinking laid the groundwork for his massive entrepreneurial success. Though best known as the outspoken owner of the Dallas Mavericks and a longtime investor on Shark Tank, Mark Cuban built his brand on bold thinking and risk-taking. His success was attributed to staying ahead of trends, betting on himself, and never being afraid to challenge the status quo.

CHAPTER FOUR
ZOOM OUT. LOCK IN.

Leaving your job is not the goal. Leaving is the result. The result of transforming into someone with a clear direction, a clear sense of identity, and a clear standard for how you want to live and work. If there is no defined path for where you're going, your journey will include building the same job you left, just in a different location, with more stress and less stability.

This is the chapter that prevents that.

These next steps matter because purpose is not poetic. Purpose is practical. It gives structure to decisions. Tells what opportunities to say yes to, what environments to be remove from, what to build, what to protect and what to refuse to tolerate anymore. Here are the lessons on how to stop reacting and start being proactive with your future.

Without a defined direction, overwhelm takes over and begins to run your life. Today marks a commitment to leave that behind. Today, the pace will slow, and the next chapter will be grounded in clarity and intention.

Why

Your Why isn't just a sentence. It is a conviction and the reason you are unable to continue to stay where you are:

> "I refuse to live a life I am simply enduring."

> "I am not here to live on autopilot."

> "My work has to mean something."

> "I am here to build, not just maintain."

Your Why is not about ambition. What's important is alignment.

What is Your Why? Write this clearly, what is the deep, underlying reason you are being called up to your next level? This is not the cute answer or socially acceptable answer. What is the true one. Even if it feels big, own it. Do not allow it to own you.

Legacy

Legacy is not about money, fame, or "impact statements."
Legacy is who you will become, what you will build, and what remains once you've moved on to whats next.

Ask yourself:

> Who am I becoming?

> What kind of life am I building?

> What will my work be known for?

> What will people gain by being in my circle?

> What will I leave better than I found it?

Your legacy is the north star. Everything else is the strategy that leads you towards your ultimate destination.

Five Year Leap
Legacy is the vision. The 5-year Leap is the direction.

This question builds your path;

If I made decisions aligned with my purpose every day for the next five years...

> Who would I be?
>
> Where would I be?
>
> What would I be doing?
>
> Who would I be doing it with?

Don't overthink it. Just say what feels slightly out of reach but undeniably yours. It should be confident, visible, and paid for with your mind, not your time. For once, choose yourself. This is not hypothetical. This version of you, at this very moment, is already forming.

One Year Focus
Where clarity becomes movement. A 50-step plan is unnecessary, just a short term directional commitment:

Over the next 12 months, what must get done?

This is an energetic and strategic boundary that moves you toward your 5-year self. If it is off-course, it is a distraction. This is protection from over-working and reinforcing aligning.

Purpose is your foundation.
Positioning is your structure.

This is the blueprint of your next chapter.

SMART QUIT REALITY CHECK

What is my Why... the real one?

Who will I be 10 years from now?

Who will I be in 5 years if I stop playing small?

What is my focus for the next 12 months?

What am I tolerating that needs to be removed?

Write it. Speak it. Own it.

Real People. Real Quits. Real Wins.

Lisa Price

Smart Quit Age: 32 years old (started Carol's Daughter in 1993 while working full-time)
Education: Attended college (did not complete degree)
Economic Background: Middle-class; working-class family (mother was a book-keeper; father was an insurance salesman)

Before Lisa Price became the founder of Carol's Daughter, a multi-million dollar natural beauty brand, she worked in TV production on the Cosby Show. Though she liked the creative energy of television, her job was demanding, the hours were long and she often felt her need for creative expression was left unfulfilled.

She started making body butters and oils as a hobby in her kitchen using essential oils and natural ingredients. Her products were so good, friends began begging to buy them. For years, Lisa ran her buzzing side business after hours, during her "5-9", making batches at night, working trade shows on weekends and fulfilling orders out of her apartment.

One day after an exhausting day on set and after another sleepless night filling product orders she was reprimanded at work for being late and though this wasn't the first time, this time it hit differently. This was her breaking point.

She was pouring everything into her dream, while her job was still treating her like she was easily replaceable. That day, she realized, if I can work this hard for someone else, I can work this hard for myself. Though terrified, she left her job determined to succeed and officially launched Carol's Daughter full time.

Her products gained a cult following, including celebrity fans. She first began selling it in stores in New York, but eventually caught the attention of national retailers.

In 2014, Carol's Daughter was acquired by L'Oreal the world's largest cosmetics and beauty company in a landmark deal. Lisa's breaking point wasn't dramatic, but it was a small moment that revealed a big truth; she was already acting like a CEO and mogul, but being held back as an employee.

CHAPTER FIVE
FIXER TO FOUNDER

Most people think entrepreneurship starts when they quit their job and start a business. It does not. Entrepreneurship starts the moment it becomes clear the work you are doing is already entrepreneurial; leading without the title, solving problems no one assigned, fixing what was broken before anyone else even noticed.

Thinking like a CEO while being paid like an employee. This chapter names that.

There was a meeting, one that's instantly memorable. It wasn't your meeting. You weren't the one who called it. You weren't the one who was supposed to lead it. Somewhere between the confusion, the questions, the half-answers, and the awkward silence… everyone turned to you. "Can you just walk us through what needs to happen?" And without hesitation, you did.

The problem got articulated. Priorities got organized. Next steps got assigned. Deadlines got clarified. Everyone left knowing exactly what to do. That wasn't luck. That wasn't personality. That wasn't "helping." That was leadership, structure, and strategy, flowing naturally from you.

Not because someone asked. That's just who you are.

The problem is that moment didn't count as evidence of capability. However, that's exactly what it was.

Experience isn't random. Everything up to this point has been shaping how you think, how you solve, how you lead, and how you create value. Your job didn't just pay, it trained.

The workplace has been a business school, leadership lab, strategic apprenticeship, and emotional intelligence gym. Not every job automatically provides those things but with strategy, these hidden lessons, tools, skills, and resources show up everywhere, every day.

The Four Core Strength Archetypes

The Four Core Strength Archetypes uncover the truth about how you operate at your best. They highlight the strengths you lean on, the patterns that drive your decisions, and the unique way you create impact. When you understand your archetype, you stop forcing yourself into roles that don't fit and start building a path that aligns with who you are at your core.

You may have elements of all four, but one is naturally more dominant one and reveals the way you are wired to win... how you think, lead, and create results. Once you identify yours, everything about your next move becomes clearer.

The Navigator
Navigators see patterns, create clarity and simplify complexity. Those with this as their dominant archetype build business models around:

    Consulting

    Advisory

    Strategic planning

    Facilitation

Systems

Operations optimization

The Trust Builder

Trust Builders read people, connect easily and create trust. Those with this dominant archetype build business models around:

Coaching

Leadership development

Community building

People-first brand development

The Systems Whisperer

System Whisperers make things work. They execute and create systems that sustain. Those with this as their dominant archetype build business models around:

Fractional Services

Process & workflow consulting

Organizational development services

The Possibility Maker

Possibility makers create new possibilities, see what doesn't exist yet and make ideas real. They build business models as the:

Founder

Creator

Brand builder

Thought leader

While your dominant archetype reveals the way you're wired to win, it's only the starting point. The next layer is your Signature Strength; the specific skill, advantage, or natural ability that consistently sets you apart. Your archetype explains how you operate; your Signature Strength clarifies what you do exceptionally well. Together, they form the blueprint for where you create the most impact and how you should position yourself in your next chapter.

Your Signature Strength is the one thing you do better than almost anyone else. These are the skill that feels effortless to you but transformational to others. It's the theme in your wins, your reputation, and your highest-value work. When you identify it and build around it, you unlock clarity, confidence, and strategic direction. Your Signature Strength becomes the anchor for your business, your brand, and the opportunities you should pursue next.

Your Signature Strength is the overlap of:

> What comes naturally

> What you consistently do well

> What others rely on you for

> What feels effortless, but leaves an impact

SMART QUIT REALITY CHECK

Answer the following:

People come to me when they need help with:

The thing I can do quickly that others overthink is:

The results I can create even under pressure are:

When I am operating at my best, I am:

Now combine your responses into this statement:

My dominant core archetype is _____________________________ and my

Signature Strength is ______________________________________,

and I use it to help ________________ solve ____________________.

____

This is the foundation of your business.
You are not just "helpful." You are skilled.
You are not just "supportive." You are strategic.
You are not "just good at figuring things out." You are a problem-solver with a repeatable, transferable process.
You have been undercharging, over-delivering, and powering entire rooms without acknowledgment. That stops here.

Say this out loud because your identity needs to hear your voice, "The value I create is real. I no longer minimize it."

Now that you know your Archetype, Signature Strength, why people trust you and the problem you solve, this is your business. This is your repeatable value engine that now just needs to be proven.

Real People. Real Quits. Real Wins.

Marie Foreleo

Smart Quit Age: 26 years old (Online newsletter & coaching business launched in 2001)
Education: B.S. in Business and Finance
Economic Background: Working-class, Italian-American family from New Jersey; father a small business owner, mother a homemaker

Before Marie Foreleo became a global brand and host of MarieTV, she was a one-woman business working as a life coach in New York. No studio, team, or fancy funnels, just her laptop and a belief that she could help people create a life and business they loved. Her first offer? A $99 coaching package that she promoted through a simple email to friends and acquaintances. No website. No social media campaigns. Just a note that said, "Here's what I can help you with. If you're interested, hit reply."

She kept it focused, personal and approachable. She was not selling a brand, she was offering value. That one email landed her a handful of clients and more importantly validated her idea. From there she slowly built a client base, raised her rates, launched group coaching and eventually scaled to online courses, a bestselling book and a multi-million dollar business.

She started small and simple. She did not have a complex platform or high overhead, just a focused offer. She leaned into authenticity as her differentiator. Her tone was direct, personal, and honest – not salesy. As she got results for clients, she revised her business and expanded.

MarieTV turned into a global platform with millions of views and subscribers. It became a digital stage that deepened Marie's connection with her audience and attracted top-tier guests like Brene Brown, Seth Godin, and Elizabeth Gilbert. Additionally, Marie's flagship online course, B-School has generated tens of millions in revenue and helped launch thousands of online businesses, making it one of the most successful online courses of its kind.

The success of Marie and MarieTV is a masterclass in personal branding, content marketing, and mission-driven entrepreneurship. Her rise wasn't about chasing fame, but about building trust, delivering value consistently and empowering her audience to believe that everything is figureoutable (yes, that's a word). She turned herself into a brand and became the engine that fueled a multi-million dollar business; one episode, one course, one transformation at a time.

**I can't tell you the key to success,
but the key to failure is trying to please everyone.**
Arthur Ashe

CHAPTER SIX
YOU'RE NOT FOR EVERYONE AND THAT'S OKAY

One of the quickest ways to drain your energy and dilute your impact is trying to build something for everyone. When you speak to everyone, no one hears you. When you try to serve everyone, no one feels deeply served. Your business is not supposed to be universal. It is supposed to be aligned. Aligned with your strengths, values, voice and the people who actually benefit from what you create.

Work has a frequency and the right people recognize it instantly. Your job isn't to convince people to want what's being offered; it's to identify the ones who already do. Your audience isn't hypothetical or "someday." It already exists: former coworkers, clients supporting behind the scenes, friends who always ask for input, people who screenshot posts, and customers who notice taste, discernment, and presence. They're already drawn to the way thinking happens, the way things are created, the way decisions are made, and the way the world is seen.

Two Types of Alignment: Identity + Utility
There are two ways people become your customer, Identity-driven and Utility-driven. Some businesses exist to transform identity or deepen purpose. Some businesses exist to solve a real, practical need.

Identity-Driven Demand
They buy because your service or product reflects:

> Who they are

> Who they are becoming

> How they want to be seen

This is common in coaching, consulting, personal brands, fashion, lifestyle, wellness, beauty, thought leadership and community-based products.

Utility-Driven Demand
They buy because your service or product:

> Solves a problem

> Saves time

> Reduces friction

> Makes life easier

> Works better than alternatives

This is common in systems, organization, operations, tools, planners, journals, templates, food and convenience services, software and apps and physical goods designed for everyday use.

Both types are valid. Both types are profitable. Both types require clarity. Your job is to know which one you are or whether you operate as a hybrid.

If you are service based, your aligned audience is the person who is already trying, already cares, already shows up, already thinks deeply and is tired of outgrowing environments that cannot meet their capacity.

They don't need motivation. They need strategy and space.

Your role is to help them become who they already are - with purpose.

If you are product-based, your aligned audience is the person who wants their daily life to reflect their identity, mood, values, or evolution, and they make purchasing decisions based on meaning, experience, or ease.

Whether you are selling apparel, candles, stationery, accessories, digital assets, home goods, lifestyle tools, your product does one of two things:

It solves something they need (utility) or
It expresses something they feel (identity)

Either is powerful. Either is enough. Either can be your business.

Here are some identity vs. utility examples.

BUSINESS TYPE	WHY THEY BUY	POSITIONING SHOULD HIGHLIGHT...
Planner Organizer	Makes life easier	Efficiency, relief, clarity, structure
Apparel Lifestyle Goods	Expresses identity or story	Mood, confidence, attitude, becoming
Coaching Consulting	Supports purpose and direction	Clarity, leadership, alignment
Services (VA, editor, designer, ops)	Saves time or reduces stress	Ease, competence, reliability

If your service or product is utility-driven, your messaging must be simple and clear. If it is identity-driven your messaging must be emotional and resonant. If its a hybrid, your messaging must do both with intention.
The next step is getting crystal clear on who needs you. Alignment within yourself is powerful, but alignment with the right audience is what turns clarity into momentum. That's where the Four Layers of Audience Clarity

come in, these layers help you define exactly who you serve, why they need you, and how to speak directly to the people who are already looking for what you offer.

Most business advice stops at demographics, but that is just surface-level positioning. To build identity-based alignment, we must go deeper.

The Four Layers of Audience Clarity

DEMOGRAPHIC - Who They Are on Paper
Age, career stage, education, income, industry
This defines the context of their life.

GEOGRAPHIC - Where They Live/Operate
City, environment, lifestyle pace
This shapes their access and experiences.

PSYCHOGRAPHIC - How They Think
Values, motivations, frustrations, desires
This defines their internal world.

SOCIOGRAPHIC - The Culture That Shaped Them
Corporate, creative, entrepreneurial, academic, faith-based, etc.
This explains their identity rules and unlearning work.

Your business sits at the intersection of these four layers.
But the center of the overlap is your sweet spot. Your audience.

The Positioning Filter

Your Strength
Their Identity
Desired
Transformation
Your Offer

Your business is not built on, "What should I sell?"
Your business is built on, Who am I speaking to, and what shift are they moving through?

Here are a couple examples of an aligned offer statement:

Service
I create strategic clarity for high-performing professionals who are ready to become entrepreneurs, so they can transition with confidence and stability.

Product
I create elevated lifestyle products for women stepping into their power, so their daily life reflects the identity they are growing into.

Same clarity.
Different delivery.
Same aligned audience.

The biggest businesses are often built on the simplest offers, delivered with clarity, consistency and courage.

SMART QUIT REALITY CHECK

Aligned Audience Statement Formula:

I create ____________ (product/service/experience)

for ____________ (identity group)

who want to ____________ (desired shift)

so they can ____________ (who they are becoming).

Real People. Real Quits. Real Wins.

Sara Blakey

Smart Quit Age: 27 years old (founded Spanx around 1999)
Education: B.S. in Communications
Economic Background: Grew up in Clearwater, Florida in a middle-class family (father a trial attorney, mother an artist)

Before Sara Blakey became the world's youngest self-made female billionaire she was selling Danka fax machines door-to-door for seven years. When the idea arose for Spanx, she didn't know anyone in the fashion or retail industries, but she pitched it the same way she sold fax machines with passion, storytelling and relentless persistence.

"Smart Quit" lessons from her fax machine job:

Sales Training: She went through an intense corporate training program at Danka, one of the largest office equipment companies at the time.

How to Handle Rejection: She heard no constantly. That job taught her how to pitch confidently, handle objections, and persist.

Cold Calling and Storytelling: She mastered how to read people, craft quick pitches and stay upbeat when doors literally slammed in her face.

Problem Solving: She learned how to think on her feet and how to sell without relying on flash – just value.

How she used it in her business:

Wrote her own patent after learning how from a 4150 patent-writing kit

Cold-called hosiery mills until someone agreed to prototype her idea

Convinced Newman Marcus to carry Spanx by pitching to the buy-

er in the bathroom where she modeled the product
Used her sales background to get Spanx into stores and eventually onto Oprah's "Favorite Things" list, skyrocketing her brand.

Sara Blakely founded Spanx with just $5,000 in savings and no formal business background, after cutting the feet off her pantyhose to solve a personal wardrobe problem. She turned that simple idea into a billion-dollar shapewear empire by bootstrapping her way into major retail stores and winning over consumers. Blakely became the youngest self-made female billionaire, celebrated for her resilience, creativity, and grit. Her success story proves that solving a real-world problem, backed by relentless determination, can lead to extraordinary results.

Sara didn't leave Danka, her last employer empty handed and neither should you! She left with real, transferable skills and tools; sales training, communications skills, confidence and most importantly: the mindset that no training is ever wasted when you know how to invest in yourself.

CHAPTER SEVEN
SIDE HUSTLE TO START UP

There are thousands of people who can do the same work you do. However, no one does it the same way. Your advantage isn't the best resume, most certifications, or perfectly polished business plan. It's in how problems are seen, how solutions are built, how decisions are made, how people are led, and how care shows up. That's what makes a business undeniable.

That "special thing" has been there for a long time; it's your edge. Long before you were even thinking about entrepreneurship. It wasn't paid for, it may not have had a name, and it may not be fully understood. It always shows up: walking into rooms with clarity others didn't have, perspective others missed, leadership others leaned on, and instincts others trusted. Your edge isn't just a learned skill. It's a unique lens.

Don't sell tasks. Sell the way thinking happens; pattern recognition, spotting inefficiencies, clarifying chaos, hearing what isn't being said, holding complexity, seeing potential before it exists, and bringing calm where others bring pressure. People don't just buy what gets done; they buy the mind behind it.

People buy who someone is, how they show up and what they stand for. This is where many employees-turned-entrepreneurs get stuck. In a job, being the fixer and the reliable "team player" earns trust and praise. In business, that same trait has to become authority, positioning, specialization, differentiation and value that gets paid for. The difference has always been there. What's missing is learning how to monetize it.

Let's name that differentiating edge Your edge is made up of three things:
Your Strength Pattern
Your Lived Experiences
Your Perspective.

Your Strength Pattern
The instinctive way you solve problems.
Examples:

You see the big picture instantly.

You notice the details no one else catches.

You know how to calm a room.

You can make a system out of anything.

You are a natural connector.

You pull the best out of people.

Your Lived Experience
These are the situations, environments, and challenges that trained your instincts. These are not your job titles, but your patterns. You didn't just work on previous jobs.
You learned:

How culture moves

How decisions are made

How to lead without authority

How to stabilize chaos

How to translate vision into execution

Your Perspective

These are your beliefs about what works, what matters, what creates change and how to move forward. This is your philosophy; the part people quote and the part people remember. Your philosophy is your brand voice.

Your business will become powerful when you stop selling what you know and start speaking from what you believe. People follow belief systems, not features.
Examples of belief statements:

> Your job is not your identity. It is your investor.

> You can transition into entrepreneurship with clarity, not chaos.

> Discipline creates freedom.

> Alignment is more powerful than ambition.

These statements are magnetic because they are true, clean, irrefutable, and make people feel seen. Your philosophy is your signature language.

Your Positioning : The Measurable Shift

Every aligned business offers a before and after, the measurable shift. It's not always dramatic or emotional. It can be as simple as more clarity, more organization, more time, more peace, more visibility, more confidence, or more alignment.

MY EDGE IS:

MY PHILOSOPHY IS:

Your Promise is the shift someone experiences after interacting with your product or service and the result. **Your Philosophy** is the why behind it. And **your Edge** is the how. Together, they form **your Positioning**.

MY PROMISE IS:

Once you understand your Promise, Philosophy, and Edge and how they come together to form your Positioning, the next step is pressure-testing it. A strong position isn't just clear on paper; it has to hold up in the real world. The 4C Startup Test helps you evaluate whether your idea is not only meaningful, but market-ready.

The 4C Startup Test

Clarity - *What do I offer?*
Clarifying your offer is crucial to ensure you are attracting the right customers and building initial momentum. A clear offer defines what you're selling, who it is for, the specific problem it solves, and the value it delivers.

How will your service or product transform the lives of your customer and how is your solution better or different than what is already available? This sets expectations, builds trusts and make it easier for your customers to say "yes." Even great ideas can get lost in the noise without clear communication of the value proposition in a way that is direct, compelling and most importantly, easy to understand.

Credibility - *Why me?*
It is essential to gain testimonials, early user feedback and case studies to demonstrate real-world results. Understand how you will earn trust from your customers, partners and investors. This will only happen with clear communication, showcasing your expertise, delivering consistent value and quality in your product and/or services.

After your first sales, users seeing your product in action and imagining how they could benefit in the same way is powerful. Align yourself with credible advisors, collaborators or even well-known platforms. Doing this "borrows" their trust while you are still building yours. Most importantly be reliable. Do what you say you will do, even if it's something small. People will begin to believe in your brand and your ability to follow through.

Customer - *Who needs this now?*
This is the most critical step in launching a business because there can be the best product, however if there are no customers , there will never be a sale and that's the entire reason to start a business, right? Once the problem is clearly defined, the focus shifts to identifying who experiences it most frequently, who is most motivated to solve it, and who has the ability to pay for the solution. Where these three overlap is the core customer base.

Customer demographics have already been defined: location, age group, race, gender, and salary range. Psychographics are also understood, including thought patterns, behaviors, goals, and pain points. This clarity makes it possible to focus on the spaces where the ideal customer already spends time; online communities, social platforms, festivals or conferences, parties, industry events, and local meetups. Engagement happens through observation, thoughtful questions, and close listening to validate assumptions before building too much. The clearer the customer understanding, the more effective the sales efforts.

Cash Flow - *How can I earn money in the next 30 days?*
Cash flow is the heartbeat of any startup, especially in the critical first 90 days. Building cash flow can and should begin before a Smart Quit. Cash flow must be monitored carefully, both incoming and outgoing, to ensure essential expenses are covered, including inventory, subscriptions, shipping, tools, and other operational needs. To generate cash quickly, fast-turnaround sales opportunities can be prioritized, such as a Kickstarter campaign or pre-selling a product. Additional options include offering early-bird discounts or securing short-term contracts. Encouraging upfront payments or deposits also helps maintain healthy cash flow. Proactive management early on sets the foundation for sustainable growth and reduces the risk of future financial trouble.

Continuing to work as part of a Smart Quit strategy while answering the 4C Test provides margin and reduces pressure during the already stressful process of starting a new business. This approach allows progress to happen in the background without disrupting an existing role.

The initial focus should remain on securing the first offer, first sale, and first client. As the business grows and becomes successful, notoriety, influence, and followers tend to follow naturally, if those outcomes are a priority.

A key question must be addressed early: Is the goal to build a side hustle, or to develop a strategic plan for a true startup? This distinction matters, as each path requires a different level of commitment, mindset, and decision-making. The answer shapes the next steps in the entrepreneurial process.

If building a side hustle, a Smart Quit should not occur until there is readiness to transition the side hustle into a startup. A side hustle is typically used for supplemental income, creative expression, or skill development. Risk levels are low, and the work can be paused or discontinued easily. While exceptions exist, side hustles usually involve modest scaling and income and often function as passion projects. Examples include freelance writing, tutoring, operating an Etsy shop, or driving for Uber or Lyft.

A startup, by contrast, is a scalable business designed for growth and market impact. Strategy centers on eventually operating full-time, often with consideration given to external funding such as investors or venture capital. Startups carry higher risk than side hustles and require greater investment of time and resources. Scaling is more aggressive, and the target market is larger. For those already in business, the visual checklist on the next page and the accompanying quiz can be used to assess readiness.

SMART QUIT REALITY CHECK

Your 4C Startup Test

What do I offer?

Why me?

Who needs my service or product right now?

How can I earn money in my business in the next 30, 60, or 90 days?

SIDE HUSTLE OR START UP
Quiz

Directions:
Answer Yes or No to each question (no "maybe").
Answer based on what's true right now, not what you hope will be true later.
Don't overthink it. Go with your first honest answer.
When you finish, count how many Yes answers you have.
Match your total to the results section to see your best next move.

Yes No

◯ ◯ Can I build and run this solo or with minimal help?

◯ ◯ Will this bring in extra income within the next 1-3 months?

◯ ◯ Can I run this while keeping my full-time job?

◯ ◯ Does this idea solve a specific need for a small niche audience?

◯ ◯ Am I okay if this never scales beyond a few $1000 per month?

◯ ◯ Am I focused on low risk and flexible time investment?

◯ ◯ Is my goal to build personal freedom, not a large team or company?

◯ ◯ Do I plan to self-fund my venture with no outside investors?

◯ ◯ Is this built around my own skills (freelance, coaching, products)?

◯ ◯ Would I still do this even if it stays small?

7+ Yes: You're leaning side hustle

Mostly No: You're leaning startup.

Real People. Real Quits. Real Wins.

Sophia Amoruso

Smart Quit Age: 22 years old (founded Nasty Gal in 2006)
Education: High school dropout; later earned a GED
Economic Background: Working-class upbringing; parents struggled financially.

While working as a security guard at the Academy of Art University, Sophia Amoruso started an eBay store called Nasty Gal Vintage. She found vintage clothes at thrift stores and estate sales and marketed them online using friends as models in cool and edgy shoots. While she remained at her security job to pay the bills, during her non-working hours she continued to build her online business scouring for hidden gems, spending hours listing, styling and shipping clothes. She taught herself photography, customer service and branding. By reinvesting all her profits back into the business it grew slowly, but steadily.

Before Shopify, Instagram and TikTok, Sophia was early to the e-commerce boom and used Myspace as her marketplace creating brand loyalty of fashion-forward, alternative women. After being shut down for a policy violation, Sophia launched NastyGal.com, her own standalone website. Nasty Gal began as an eBay store selling vintage clothing and quickly grew into a fashion empire. Within just a few years, the company scaled to over $100 million in revenue and earned a loyal following of young, trend-savvy shoppers. Sophia was soon after named one of the richest self-made women in the world.

Sophia didn't have a fancy job or even work in the fashion industry before launching her fashion business. However, her "boring" job funded her multi-million dollar empire because she had hustle, was consistent and knew how to manage her time and resources well.
Sophia was hailed as a millennial business icon and celebrated in Forbes "30 under 30", praised for her #GIRLBOSS ethos.

At the same time, behind the scenes, the company scaled too fast. The team grew to over one hundred employees and operational costs exploded. Sophia was a first-time CEO navigating high-growth territory without the infrastructure or leadership experience to match the speed of expansion. The brand went from lean and scrappy to corporate and chaotic. Key executives left. Customer service failed. Fast fashion competitors began to outpace the company with cheaper prices and faster delivery.

Six years after raising millions in funding, Nasty Gal filed for bankruptcy. In interviews after the collapse, Sophia candidly shared that the company scaled too fast and didn't build the necessary foundation. They grew way before they were ready. Thankfully Sophia was able to bounce back later rebuilding her personal brand and launching Girlboss Media. She used the experience to fuel conversation around leadership and sustainable growth and the true cost of hyper scaling. You too can learn from Sophia's experience and not repeat the same mistakes when launching your business.

Sophia's story isn't about failure. It's about learning the hard way that fast growth isn't always smart growth. It's a real-world example why the goal isn't to move fast; it's to move smart so your success is sustainable, not accidental or fragile.

CHAPTER EIGHT
YOUR VALUE NEEDS A HOME

Clarity without structure doesn't create revenue. And purpose without packaging doesn't create momentum. We must now refine the container for what you bring, who it's for and the way it works. Your initial offer.

Your offer is simply:

> The solution,

> The way people access the transformation,

> Or the experience you create.

That's it. An offer is not complicated even though people are often trained to overthink offers.

The Aligned Offer Framework

Your offer must do three things:

1. Solve a Real Problem
Not a theoretical problem. An actual problem. Ask the question, "What is the thing your client/customers are tired of struggling with?"

2. Deliver a Clear Win

Your client/customer should be able to say, "This helped me by ______." Fill in the blank with; bringing clarity, providing relief, building confidence, increasing efficiency and ease, creating identity, or strengthening stability. That's the win.

3. Be Sustainable for You

If it drains you, it is not the right offer. If it overloads your schedule, it is not aligned. If it requires constant force, it is not ready. Your business should not be meant to break you.

An offer must match its founder's season. Most owners design their business backwards asking, "What is a good offer to sell?" and end up creating something they don't have the time, energy, capacity, skill or audience for yet. That leads to overwhelm, inconsistency, and eventually shutdown.

An offer should come from one question, what is the simplest and most aligned way to create a clear win for my audience right now... in the life I actually have? Not in a life you wish you had. Not in a future version of your schedule. Not in your post-quitting dream scenario. This life. This capacity. This season.

Before choosing your initial offer, it is important to identify which founder season you are in;

    Foundation Season
    Expansion Season
    Ownership Season

Foundation Season

Still on the job and making moves. This is the Foundation Season where identity, clarity, and proof are stacked, and discipline and visibility get real. Keep the offer simple, flexible, and easy to deliver. Smart progress, zero chaos.

Examples:

    1:1 service

Small batch product drops

Digital or downloadable product

Workshops / small events

Product prototypes / test runs

A Smart Quit most often begins in the Foundation Season, a phase focused on building evidence and rhythm.

Expansion Season
Demand is real. Results, testimonials, and proof of customer interest are in place. Expansion Season is the time to level up: raise the price, deepen the offer, and scale with support systems
Examples:

Group programs

Higher-tier product lines

Membership/community models

Recurring product collections

Signature frameworks + trainings

You are building systems and consistency.

Ownership Season
Voice is owned, brand identity is strong, and market positioning is understood. In the Ownership Season, licensable frameworks, scalable assets, distribution channels, and partnerships are built to expand the brand.
Examples:

Digital Courses

Books/ workbooks

Brand partnerships

Product lines/expanded SKUs

Corporate training/workshops

Here is where legacy takes shape. The Ownership Season isn't the start of entrepreneurship; it's the point of mastery.

Here's a truth to stand on. A website, a logo, a brand shoot, a funnel or a team to start, though all are great, none are needed. All that is needed is a clear audience, a clear offer, a clear result and a clear way to receive payment. Everything else is just a distraction or decoration.

Once the offer framework is clear, the next step is proving it in the market. A **Minimum Viable Product (MVP)** tests an offer quickly, gathers real feedback, and validates demand before investing time, energy, or money building the full version.

To find the MVP to launch a business use this Formula:

PAIN POINT	PROMISE	PROCESS	PRICE
What are they struggling with?	What's the transformation?	What's your method?	What's it worth to solve this now?

An MVP isn't about perfection, it's about proof. Before investing in ads, software, or fancy funnels, the first test is simple: understand the real pain of the customer and designing a process that actually transforms frustration into results.

This isn't built through complexity, it's done through focus. The goal is to validate demand with the least amount of effort and investment possible. That means resisting the urge to overbuild and instead prioritizing the single insight that determines whether the business moves forward: does this solve a real problem someone cares enough to pay for?

That clarity starts with the customer's pain point. Creating the first sales funnel doesn't require ads or technology, only awareness. Identify the problem showing up most consistently, shape messaging around the promise of transformation, and design a simple process to deliver it. Map the journey from the first moment awareness is created to the point where customers become loyal advocates.

Begin by defining how the product or service will be delivered. These are the operational requirements of the process. Next, assess the additional resources needed; people, financial capital, tools, or physical products. Beyond delivery, consider the internal infrastructure required to support the business. While delivery happens externally, internal systems and resources ensure the product remains viable and sustainable.

Zone of Genius Audit

ASK YOURSELF:

What lights me up and gets my best results?

What drains me, even if I'm good at it?

What could someone else do faster, better, cheaper?

Next, establish the pricing structure. Pricing should reflect the value of solving this problem now, while aligning with the target market's ability to pay. Start small and test demand through direct outreach; DMs, targeted emails, or warm introductions. When interest appears, schedule a short discovery call to better understand needs and refine the offer. Deeper customer insight allows for stronger positioning and more effective refinement.

Finally, focus energy on the core strengths that move the business forward and outsource the rest. The most valuable contribution should remain front and center. Building a company does not require becoming an assistant to every task. As soon as resources allow, delegate responsibilities that fall outside core strengths or drain energy, creating space for higher-impact work.

The Aligned Offer Framework brings focus, the Founder Season builds the foundation, and the MVP provides proof. Together, they turn ideas into action without unnecessary risk or overwhelm. This chapter closes with momentum already in place; an offer rooted in real demand, built with intention, and tested in the market before the leap is made. Progress isn't rushed; it's earned. And from here, every next move is strategic.

Real People. Real Quits. Real Wins.

Melanie Perkins

Smart Quit Age: Mid-20s (co-founded Canva in 2012)
Education: Studied Communications, Psychology (did not complete degree)
Economic Background: Middle-class upbringing; mother a teacher, father an engineer.

Melanie Perkins', co-founder of Canva, entrepreneurial journey began while she was a graphic design teacher at the University of Western Australia. She recognized that her students were struggling with complex design software like InDesign and Adobe Photoshop because the software had steep learning curves and wasn't user friendly, in addition to being expensive. She identified there was a huge gap in the market for a simple, intuitive design tool that even someone with no formal design training could use.

Using what she learned as a teacher, she bootstrapped Fusion Books from her mother's living room, launching it as an online tool and quickly proving in the real world that people wanted an easier way to design and were willing to pay for it.

Melanie was rejected by over 100 venture capitalists in Silicon Valley, because many didn't believe a simple design tool could compete with her "giant" competitors. After struggling to build the platform, it took her and her co-founder years to find the right technical partner, a former Google engineer, who brought the necessary technical expertise and helped build a scalable product. With limited resources, they hired a global remote team to develop and design the Minimum Viable Product. The team built Canva from the ground up, focusing on simplicity, speed and usability.

After years of pitching investors and refining her concept, Melanie and her co-founders launched Canva which took off almost immediately thanks to its clean interface, wide selection of templates and drag-and drop features.

Within the first year, Canva had over 750,000 users to confirm a strong product-market fit.

Today, everyone including students, small business and Fortune 500 companies use Canva in over 190 countries and the company is valued at over $25 billion. Melanie became one of the youngest self-made female billionaires.

Melanie paid close attention to a common problem in her everyday work as a teacher and had the creativity, determination and persistence to create a product and business to solve it on a global scale.

Stage Two:
POSITION

**Your life does not get better by chance
it gets better by change.**
Jim Rohn

CHAPTER NINE
TIMING IS EITHER STRATEGY OR SELF-SABOTAGE

Leaving a job is not an emotional event. It is a strategic transition. Your exit should feel steady, grounded, clear, and intentional, not rushed, chaotic, or dramatic. Stability does not have to be sacrificed to chase freedom. Stability funds freedom. Your job is never the enemy, it is your biggest investor. An investor is never left early, only wisely.

The three types of "Quits"
>The Emotional Quit
>The Forced Quit
>**The Smart Quit.**

The Emotional Quit
Frustrated, burnt out, overwhelmed, or over it.
You slam the laptop shut and walk out.
This leads to chaos.

The Forced Quit
Layoffs, reorganization and leadership turnover.
You didn't choose it, but the door closed.
This leads to scrambling to survive.

The Smart Quit
Leaving when:

> Self-awareness is clear

> The audience is defined

> The offer is solid

> A runway is in place

> A plan exists

> The exit is grounded, not reactive

This leads to sustainability.
You are ready to make a Smart Quit.

The Four Readiness Indicators

1. Identity Has Shifted – The job is no longer seen as home, only as a current funding source. There is no resentment. No bitterness. Just a sense that growth there is complete.

2. Signature Strength Is Clear – The value brought to the table is obvious, without needing a job title to validate it.

3. Offer Delivers a Real Win – The solution may not be perfect or fully scaled yet, but it's proven to work for someone beyond the founder.

4. Financial Runway Exists – A defined, realistic plan covers saving, cutting unnecessary expenses, and replacing a portion of income before departure. This isn't a leap off a cliff; it's a bridge being built.

The question everyone asks is, "How is it possible to know for sure?"

The truth: certainty doesn't exist. There is no permission slip, no sign, no guarantee. However peace can replace fear, direction can replace confusion, and clarity can replace anxiety. A Smart Quit is not impulsive, it happens when staying starts costing more than leaving ever could. Not just financially, but spiritually, psychologically, and emotionally. Your soul is asking for more.

This exit isn't just about leaving. It's about reclaiming energy, repositioning time, redirecting talent, reinstating voice, and redistributing loyalty back to self. This is not leaving a job; this is returning to essence.

A leap without preparation is chaos. Before resigning, the foundation must be solid. Build first, then say goodbye.

On the timeline:

Clarify who is being served

Finalize the offer

Establish a minimum revenue bridge

Shift the calendar

Exit when stability is transferring, not disappearing

This is the path to leaving confidently, not scrambling.

SMART QUIT REALITY CHECK

Emotionally: Am I leaving because I'm done growing, or because I'm tired?

Practically: What is the bare minimum income I need to maintain stability?

Strategically: Brainstorm additional offers that can replace a portion of that income.

Energetically: What is the real cost of staying where I am?

The truth is already inside._______________
This is the language just unlocks it.

Real People. Real Quits. Real Wins.

Anthony Wood

Smart Quit Age: 20s (founded first entrepreneurial ventures)
Education: Bachelor's Degree, Electrical Engineering
Economic Background: Grew up internationally

Anthony Wood's Smart Quit™ was a strategic handoff from employee leverage to founder leverage. By the time Roku happened, he wasn't new to building. He'd already created ReplayTV, one of the early DVR pioneers, and had learned the hard lesson that innovation alone doesn't win. You also have to understand industry dynamics.

Then came the move that makes his story the perfect Smart Quit: he took a job for purpose. In 2007, Wood joined Netflix as Vice President of Internet TV to push a streaming player project through production. His goal was not to go corporate, but to get closer to the future. He used his role to sit at the center of the exact problem he wanted to solve: how people would stream content to their TVs.

After about 10 months, he left Netflix. The job wasn't bad, but opportunities were bigger outside the building than inside it. Here's the key Smart Quit™ detail: when he left, Netflix spun Project Griffin into Roku and became an early investor. That's what it looks like to exit clean: relationships intact, credibility earned, and momentum transferred.

Roku launched its first set-top box in 2008, and Wood made a different set of decisions than in his earlier venture: keep hardware prices low, make setup simple, and win by being the easiest bridge between streaming services and the living room. Over time, Roku expanded beyond dongles into an operating system embedded in TVs and then into the higher-margin business that powers the modern streaming economy: advertising and platform distribution.

This Smart Quit™ lesson is to use the job as a strategic classroom, step into proximity with real problems, and then leave when you have a clear platform to build. Wood didn't burn the bridge, he turned it into a runway.

CHAPTER TEN
THE REAL-WORLD MBA

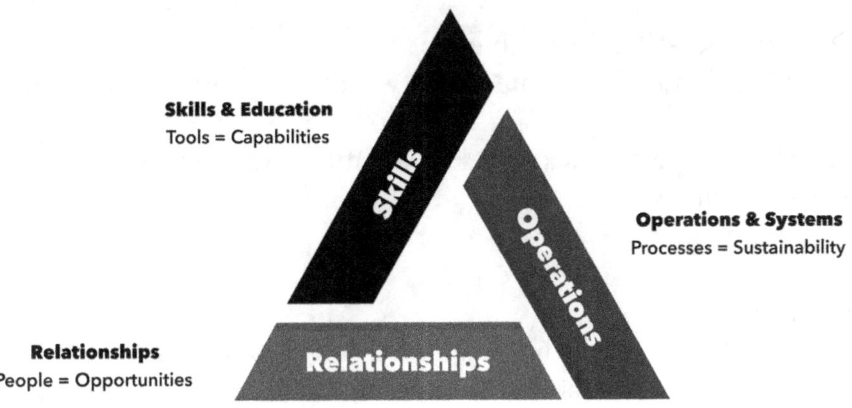

Most people think quitting a job is a single event; one conversation with HR, one resignation letter, one leap into the unknown. Smart Quitting isn't a moment; it's a build, a transition, a transformation. If done correctly, Smart Quitters deliberately create of a new identity; one prepared, equipped, and positioned to win on the entrepreneurial side.

Think of a career like a house. A job provides a solid foundation, maybe even a beautiful structure. Entrepreneurship? That's building a new addition, sometimes from the ground up. The biggest mistake is moving into the new space before it's framed, wired, insulated, and livable.

The Smart Quit Pyramid is the design. It shows how to build the pillars of a sustainable transition, so no leap from salary into chaos, or from comfort into confusion. The door is walked out ready, resourceful, and recession-proof.

The Smart Quit Pyramid™

Layer One: Relationships
People who accelerate opportunity and open doors.

Layer Two: Skills + Education
Tools that expand capability, credibility, and competence.

Layer Three: Operational Readiness
Systems and processes that create stability, scalability, and sustainability.

Together, they shape the next-level of identity, entrepreneurial readiness, and the Smart Quit runway.

Why a Pyramid?
Entrepreneurial success isn't balanced on a single factor. Networking alone won't create a thriving business without skills. Skill-stacking won't build longevity without operations. Operational structure falls flat without people who trust the business enough to work with it, hire it, or refer it.

Like a pyramid, strength comes from integration. Remove one layer, and the structure weakens. Build all three, and the foundation becomes undeniable.

This pyramid isn't theory. It's risk protection, income preservation, and confidence creation.

Relationships: *The Bridge to Opportunity*

Every major opportunity in business connects back to people. Clients are people. Mentors are people. Investors, referrals, partnerships, collaboration, all people.

Traditional jobs train the mind to think that competence is enough. Entrepreneurship teaches quickly: relationships move revenue.

Imagine entering a new business with a bench of supporters instead of a blank slate. Not begging for clients, but responding to DMs. Not chasing leads, but fulfilling requests. That's the power of relational capital. Money moves at the speed of trust. The more trust, the shorter the runway.

Smart Quit reveals who belongs in the corner, how to create opportunity-rich relationships, and how to build a network before it's needed. Do not wait until after the paycheck stops.

Skills + Education: *Your Capability Engine*

Skills are not just talent, they are currency. The marketplace pays for solutions, not passion alone. You might be gifted, talented, even brilliant but entrepreneurship demands value that can be packaged, communicated, and delivered.

Education fills the gaps, skills sharpen the sword. Together, they increase your price point.

Smart Quit looks at the difference between business skills and entrepreneurial skills, the education that actually increases earning power and how to turn knowledge into offers and offers into income. Leaving a job without marketable skills is not a launch, it's a gamble.

Smart Quitters identify what they already have, what needs refinement, and where to upskill strategically, not endlessly.

Operational Readiness: *The Sustainability System*

This is where dreams often die. The passion or talent exists, but from the business side is never built. Clients can be gained without operations, but they cannot be retained without them. Operations are the hidden structure that makes entrepreneurship feel like freedom instead of a frantic hustle.

It includes simple but crucial elements like:
>Systems for communication, delivery, and invoicing
>Boundaries, workflow, and customer experience
>The structure and processes that turn scrambling into scaling

Hustle builds income, but operations build momentum. Smart Quit breaks down how to operationalize a business before an exit, so the first month doesn't feel like survival mode. When relationships, skills, education and operational readiness align; identity shifts.

The Smart Quit Pyramid isn't only about skills or processes; it's about who you become through the build. As you strengthen relationships, expand capability, and establish operations, something shifts inside you: You stop asking "Can I do this?" and start saying "I was built for this."

That shift is your real exit strategy. Not the date. Not the resignation letter. Not even the business launch. Identity is what will carry you across the bridge. The pyramid is how we build that identity brick by brick.

Where We Go Next

In the pages ahead, each layer of the Smart Quit Pyramid will be explored in detail. First up: Skills & Education, how to build influence, create opportunity flow, and establish a runway of support before leaving a job. Next comes Operations & Systems, showing how to build the structure that turns hustle into scalable momentum. Finally, Relationships, how to cultivate trust, grow relational capital, and ensure a network is in place before the leap.

Together, these layers create a foundation for a Smart Quit that is intentional, resilient, and risk-aware. Each section builds on the last, guiding a transition from scrambling to strategic, from reactive to ready. By the end, the pyramid isn't theory, it's your playbook for moving from stagnation to growth without chaos or compromise.

By the end of these three chapters, readiness isn't a guess. It's clear.
The exit path is visible.
Your new identity is already taking shape.
When the day comes to walk out the door, it won't be a leap. It will be a step into a future already built.

Real People. Real Quits. Real Wins.

Eric Yuan

Smart Quit Age: 41 (Zoom founded in 2011)
Education: B.S. in Applied Mathematics and Master's degree in Engineering
Economic Background: No U.S. network; immigrant path with repeated visa rejections."

Eric Yuan's Smart Quit™ was a decision to stop accepting compromises. He spent 14 years inside the video-conferencing world, living with the pain points customers complained about every day. He joined WebEx as one of the early hires, watched it scale, and after Cisco acquired WebEx, he rose into senior leadership. From the outside, it was the definition of "made it": high pay, prestige, and a seat at the table.

However, the job came with a frustration that mattered. Yuan believed video meetings should feel effortless; fast, stable, and built for the reality of modern work (mobile, global, always-on). Inside Cisco, he pushed for a rebuild that would prioritize user experience. When that vision wasn't going to happen the way he believed it needed to, he made the hard call. He decided to leave the comfort of a powerful role to build the product himself.

In 2011, Yuan walked away from his executive position at Cisco and started building Zoom, initially with a team that followed him out the door. That move wasn't reckless, it was conviction backed by mastery. He wasn't guessing at the problem; he'd been living it for years. He also didn't have an easy path into the U.S. tech world. He'd tried repeatedly to get a visa and failed eight times before finally making it to Silicon Valley in 1997. So, he knew how to persist through closed doors.

The early days were not glamorous. Investors told him the market was crowded and the winners were already chosen. He built anyway, product-first, customer-first. Zoom launched publicly in 2013 and grew into a category leader because it delivered what users actually wanted: fewer dropped calls, simpler joining, and a meeting experience that didn't punish people for trying to collaborate.

Then the success became undeniable. Zoom's IPO in 2019 was one of the standout tech debuts of that year. During the pandemic, Zoom didn't just grow, it became the infrastructure for work, school, healthcare, and daily life. Yuan's Smart Quit™ wasn't "quit to find yourself." It was "quit to build what customers deserved"and then scale it with relentless attention to user happiness.

**Doing the best at this moment
puts you in the best place for the next moment.**
Oprah Winfrey

CHAPTER ELEVEN
EMPLOYEE TO EXPERT

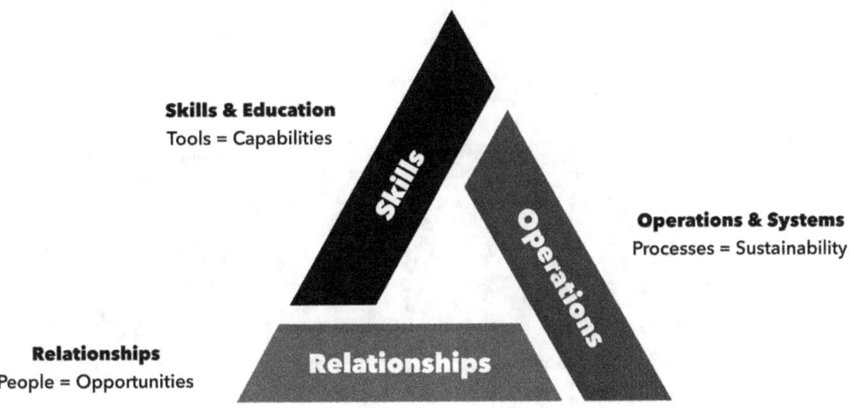

Smart Quitters aren't just working a job. They're gathering resources, learning the systems, behaviors, and patterns that make companies succeed... or fail. Every day brings exposure to future clients, collaborators, mentors, partners, employees, and referrals. It's real-time training and development on someone else's dime. A living business case study.

The next three chapters show how to recognize it, extract it, and turn it into a runway strong enough to carry you to success, without fear, chaos, or guesswork.

Smart Quitters doesn't demonize the workplace; they leverage it.

Entrepreneurship demands skill, discipline, and mastery. These are qualities most people try to learn after leaving a job, when stakes are highest and pressure is real. Smart Quitters take the opposite approach: the job becomes a university, the employer an investor, and every project a training ground. Free education, real-world experience, leadership development, and certifications are all being earned in advance; things that would cost thousands once employment ends.

The truth is simple. Your current job is preparing you for your next venture whether it's noticed or not. Every meeting, decision, mistake, achievement, and challenge builds the skillset the business will demand later. This chapter helps identify, extract, and maximize those skills so the next chapter begins prepared, not panicked.

Smart Quit Skill Extraction

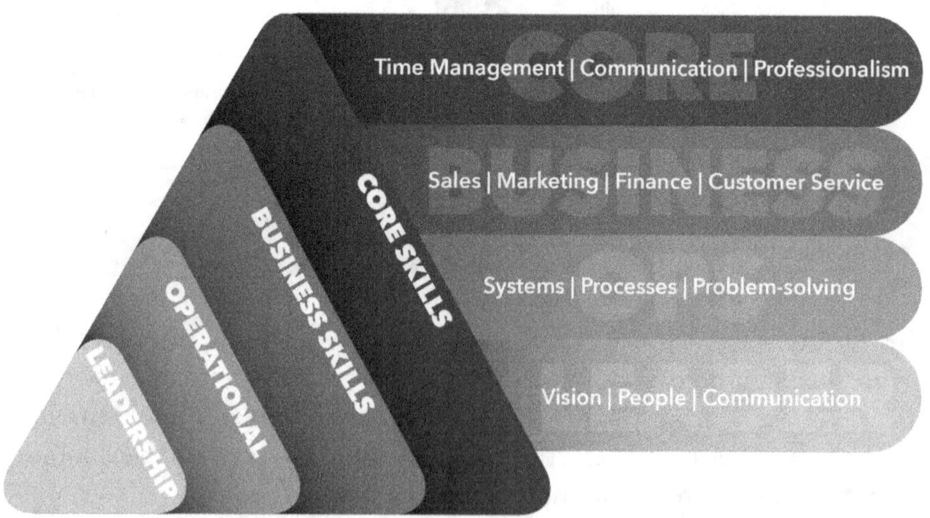

Skills are extracted from the bottom up and leveraged from the top down. Most people believe entrepreneurship requires some magical set of talents not yet possessed. The truth is, the majority of needed skills already exist, they just haven't been fully recognized or organized. The Skill Extraction Pyramid™ helps identify the layers of capability being built inside a current job and shows how to intentionally extract, strengthen, and apply them to your next chapter. Instead of leaving a job feeling unprepared, this approach creates a deep understanding of existing abilities, while identifying what still needs development.

At the base of the pyramid are Core Skills: time management, communication, professionalism, problem-solving, and reliability. These fundamentals aren't glamorous, but they earn trust, promotions, and respect. Most entrepreneurial breakdowns happen because this layer is skipped or underestimated. Smart Quitters refine these skills until they become second nature.

Above Core Skills are Business Skills. These skills are directly tied to how money moves: sales, marketing, finance, client experience, and project execution. Business skills play out daily within a company, whether noticed or not. Learning them now, while someone else covers the bills, will position you to run your business with precision rather than confusion. This layer turns talent into revenue.

Next are Operational Skills: systems thinking, process creation, workflow design, and the ability to make work easier, cleaner, and more predictable. This separates side hustles from real companies. Operations is the quiet engine that keeps everything moving. Mastering this layer before leaving ensures a business that doesn't burn out the founder.

At the top are Leadership Skills: the ability to lead yourself and others, make decisions, communicate vision, and hold standards. Leadership isn't a title; it's a skillset practiced in every meeting, project, and conflict. Strengthening this layer allows entry into entrepreneurship not just as a founder, but as a trusted leader.

The Skill Extraction Pyramid proves that no one starts from zero. The layers needed for entrepreneurial success are already being built, they just need intentional extraction. Understanding this pyramid replaces doubt with preparation for your next chapter.

Your current role is the cheapest, most resourced learning environment ever available. While most treat jobs like cages, Smart Quitters treat them like classrooms. Surrounding systems, strategies, tools, and training programs often cost companies tens of thousands of dollars. Accessing them while still earning a paycheck is a rare advantage. Shifting your perspective from restriction to preparation unlocks value most people never notice.

These are skills rarely taught in school but demanded in entrepreneurship: execution, communication, leadership, decision-making, and operational thinking. The workplace is already teaching these lessons every day. Your job is an investor. Your job is a university. Your job is a training ground, but only if approached that way.

Leveraging Employee-Paid Development

Credentials that increase authority

Proof you're the real deal

TRAINING → CERTIFICATIONS → MASTERY → CREDIBILITY → DEMAND

Employer-paid development

Practice inside your job before action inside your business

Expertise that attracts clients or customers when you Smart Quit

Most employees never use the development dollars allocated to them. Smart Quitters help companies use every dollar and every cent. From tuition reimbursement to external workshops to professional development stipends to conferences; your company is prepared to invest in your growth, often all you have to do is ask, but must be intentional and proactive.

Project management certifications, leadership courses, coaching programs, strategy training, tech certifications; these become the backbone of professional credibility when you're no longer attached to a company name. Smart Quitters use their employer's resources to build their entrepreneurial resume quietly and strategically.

Certifications instantly increase credibility when stepping into a new business or career. Once a job is left, however, those same certifications become expensive and time-consuming. A current role often provides access to continuing education budgets, leadership academies, conferences, workshops, and skill-based certifications, resources that cost thousands out of pocket later. This is the moment to acquire credentials that will give a future business authority.

This isn't about taking random classes for the sake of activity. It's about aligning development so it benefits your current role and company while adding value to your future business model. If selling will be required, sales training is important now. If leadership or project ownership will be required, leadership training is prioritized now. Future competence is being built with your existing employer resources.

Entrepreneurship demands specific competencies. Smart Quitters identify those requirements early and create a plan to close the gaps long before submitting a resignation. A Skill Gap Plan clarifies what needs to be learned, how to learn it, and where to practice it within the current role.

Approaching development strategically reduces overwhelm during the transition later. A business isn't built on passion alone, it's built on execution. Closing skill gaps early is what creates stability in the first year of entrepreneurship instead of calamity.

The Skill Gap Sprint Plan

The Skills Gap Sprint Plan turns development into progress. By identifying what matters, prioritizing what moves the needle, sprinting with intention, applying skills in real time, and documenting the results, learning stops being theoretical and starts compounding. Each sprint builds confidence, capability, and evidence. This is proof that progress is already underway. This is how preparation becomes leverage, and how skill-building turns into a strategic advantage rather than a someday goal.

Every meeting, every project, every initiative you touch holds value. Lessons about how businesses operate are everywhere. Smart Quitters pay attention to the why behind decisions, the how behind workflows, and the what behind outcomes. This is the art of extraction. Understanding how a company works makes it possible to replicate the strongest elements inside a future business.

Instead of getting frustrated with processes, they're treated as case studies. Observe how teams coordinate, how leaders lead, how projects move forward, and how decisions are made. This is business infrastructure in real time. What works gets documented. What doesn't gets documented too. Over time, this becomes a future guidebook.

Ethical boundaries do matter. The goal is to extract skills, insights, and principles, not your company's intellectual property. Proprietary documents, internal frameworks, client lists, pricing models, and confidential strategies are never copied or repurposed. Nothing is illegally downloaded or duplicated. The focus stays on patterns, best practices, successes, and failures, translating those lessons into original systems and philosophies. Smart Quitters build from wisdom, not theft. Integrity remains a non-negotiable asset.

When systems, frameworks, insights, and strategies are documented and reinterpreted through an original lens, the foundation of a business methodology begins to form. This is how consultants, strategists, coaches, and service providers develop signature frameworks. What's learned now becomes their intellectual property later.

Strategically, professional wisdom is being translated into original language and structure. Often, that documentation can evolve into a future course, program, book, or high-ticket offer.

Smart Quitters understand that entrepreneurship can be skillsets rearranged with entrepreneurial decision-making layered on top. On-the-job training is already doing much of the preparation, value simply needs to be extracted. Skills compound. Knowledge compounds. Credibility compounds. Everything learned now becomes a resource that reduces stress, accelerates revenue, and builds stability later. A strategic exit doesn't leave with only a dream. Smart Quit to leave with discipline, capability, and the competence to sustain it.

No one wants to start from scratch. Smart Quit teaches how to start from experience. The primary question to answer is how to extract as much value as possible before walking away.

SMART QUIT REALITY CHECK

What employer-paid resources am I not using right now (certifications, tuition reimbursement, conferences, leadership programs, coaching) Which one would create the biggest ROI for my next chapter?

What credential would most increase my credibility or earning power outside my current company, and can I get it covered (fully or partially) through current benefits?

What leadership skill do I need next (delegation, accountability, conflict, decision-making, coaching) and where can I get real reps at work in the next 90 days?

Do I understand how my current company actually makes money (revenue, margins, cash flow, sales cycle)? If not, what specific access can I request to learn it?

What operational system am I building right now (process, metrics, meetings, issue-solving) and how can I document it so it becomes a reusable playbook for my future business?

Real People. Real Quits. Real Wins.

Kevin Systrom

Smart Quit Age: 26 (Instagram launched in 2010).
Education: B.S., Management Science & Engineering
Economic Background: Upper-middle-class/professional household

Kevin Systrom's Smart Quit™ wasn't an emotional breakup with corporate life. It was a calculated move from resume-building to ownership-building. He had the dream track: Stanford, a coveted role at Google, and the kind of stability that convinces people to "just stay a few more years." But he wasn't looking for comfort, he was looking for control and creation.

Instead of quitting and hoping for inspiration, he started building while he still had a paycheck. The first product, Burbn, was a messy, overstuffed check-in app with too many features. And this is where the Smart Quit™ muscle shows up. He didn't fall in love with the work he'd already done. He paid attention to what users actually wanted. The signal was clear, people cared most about the photo-sharing.

So he did the thing most people avoid: he quit his wrong idea. He stripped the product down to one core behavior, rebuilt around simplicity, and launched Instagram in 2010.

The growth validated the decision fast. Instagram didn't crawl, it sprinted. Early adoption was immediate, turning it from a side project into a real platform almost overnight. And then the bigger proof arrived: in 2012, Facebook acquired Instagram for $1 billion. That wasn't just a payday, it was a market verdict that the pivot was right.

Systrom stayed after the acquisition and continued scaling the product into a global habit. Under his leadership, Instagram evolved from a simple photo app into one of the most influential consumer platforms of its generation. By June 20, 2018, Instagram announced it had reached 1 billion monthly active users, a level of scale reserved for the biggest products on Earth.

This Smart Quit™ lesson isn't "quit your job and everything works out." It's sharper than that: keep the job long enough to learn, build, and test. Then exit with a real signal. Once the signal is there, quit what's bloated, quit what's unclear, quit what's not working, so the right thing has room to win.

CHAPTER TWELVE
PROCESS OVER PRESSURE

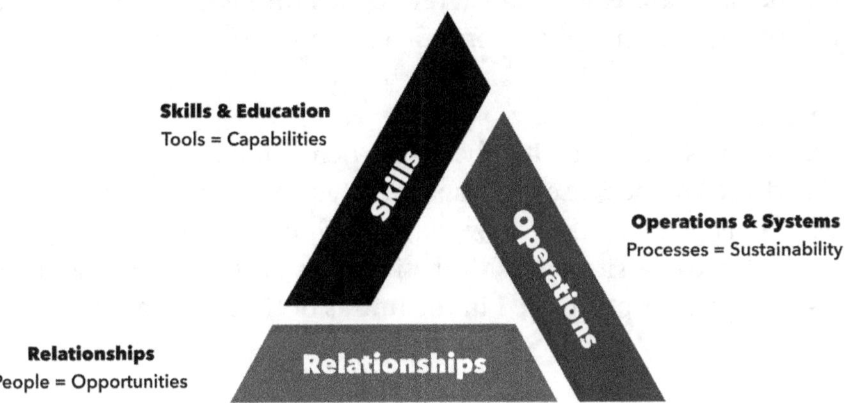

Most new entrepreneurs fail not from a lack of passion, but from a lack of operational competence. Every company either models how a future business should function or reveals exactly what not to do. Smart Quitters gain a firsthand view of a working business, knowing that what's observed today will be applied later. Decision-making, team collaboration, project flow, money movement, and leadership in action all become invaluable data. Observed from the inside, these experiences are converted into operational intelligence.

Your job is a living business case study. Every system, workflow, breakdown, meeting, and success offers insight into how companies run and how they fall apart. Before building a business, the smartest move is studying one already in motion. This chapter trains observation, analysis, and the conversion of operational insight into a framework for the next chapter.

Most employees only see the portion of the business they touch. Smart Quitters zoom out. When a company is viewed as a living organism, full of moving parts, systems, and interdependent functions, how businesses truly operate becomes clear. That perspective creates a significant advantage.

Your current role is a front-row seat to business infrastructure. What works, what breaks, what scales, and what collapses are all visible in real time. This isn't just task execution, it's studying the entire machine.

Every business, regardless of industry, operates through six core functions: marketing, sales, delivery, operations, finance, and leadership.

Marketing
Marketing creates demand. It's the story being told, the message being shaped, and the method used to capture attention. Observing what resonates, what fails, which channels work, and which messages stick provides direction for future positioning. Marketing goes far beyond ads and social posts. It's how value is positioned in the minds of those being served.

Sales
Sales is the bridge between interest and income. It turns attention into revenue. Inside any company, deals are being built, negotiated, closed, or lost every day. Sales teaches timing, relationships, objections, and confidence. No business survives without it.

Delivery
Delivery is how promises are fulfilled. It ensures customers receive what they paid for consistently, professionally, and predictably. Expectations, deadlines, communication, quality control, and experience all live here.

Businesses succeed or fail in delivery. Successful Smart Quitters master this layer early.

Operations
Operations are the backbone of any business: systems, workflows, processes, and rhythms that keep everything moving orderly. Observing operations reveals how work actually gets done, where bottlenecks appear, and which structures create efficiency. Operations turns hustles into a real companies and burnout into scalability.

Finance
Finance is your reality check. It governs cash flow, funding decisions, forecasting, and sustainability. Budgets, approvals, and cost management are always in motion, whether noticed or not. Understanding this function early prevents one of the most common entrepreneurial failures, making emotional decisions instead of data-driven financial ones.

Leadership
Leadership shapes culture, communication, direction, motivation, and accountability. Effective leadership and destructive leadership are on display every day in the workplace and both are powerful teachers. Leadership moves people, influences outcomes, and sets standards. Success in entrepreneurship isn't just running a business; it's leading one.

Right now, every company offers insight into all six functions. Whether recognized or not, whether positive or not, the full business ecosystem is already visible. Smart Quitters take time to understand how demand is created, revenue is generated, customers are served, systems operate, money flows, and leadership drives culture. Knowing these functions before quitting your current job makes entrepreneurship feel familiar instead of foreign.

Every organization constantly provides data; success patterns, inefficiencies, breakdowns, and bottlenecks. These observations become lessons that shape smoother businesses later. Failed systems, effective leaders, and collapsing processes all offer valuable information.

It's all about real-world learning, not theory. Business wisdom is being absorbed long before costly mistakes ever need to be made.

Systems are the backbone of every successful company. They dictate how work is done, how efficiently things move, and how sustainable growth becomes. Smart Quitters study workflows, SOPs, communication rhythms, operational sequences, approval processes, and cross-department coordination. Learning to think in systems now builds companies that run limiting turbulence later.

Leadership, too, is learned through proximity. Current workplaces offer daily exposure to leadership styles, patterns, and failures. Smart Quitters study what to model and what to abandon.

There's no need to wait for a founder title to act like one. Entrepreneurial behaviors such as ownership, process improvement, efficiency creation, initiative leadership, and results-driven execution, can all begin inside a job. That's how preparation turns into a strategic edge.

The Operational Observation Loop™

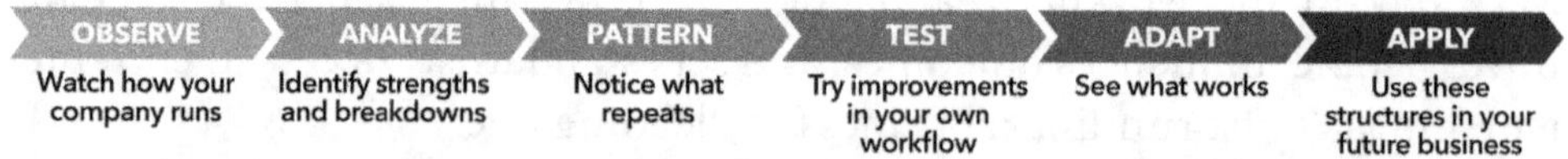

The Operational Observation Loop gives real-time practice into running a business. Confidence grows and an identity forms as someone capable of running a business long before launching one. Observations become a blueprint: consolidating what's learned about systems, client experience, and team operations lays the foundation for the future company. This blueprint evolves into your first SOPs, processes, delivery model, and operational approach.

Entrepreneurs who skip this step struggle. Smart Quitters build these concepts while still employed, entering entrepreneurship with a head start instead of a handicap. Some of the most stable businesses are founded by those who took time to understand how a previous company operated.

They didn't rush out of frustration, they extracted wisdom, observed patterns, and applied best practices. Success followed naturally as a result of their attention and intention.

The Owner's Manual Blueprint:
Build the systems your business will run on before you quit.

SYSTEMS	STRUCTURES	STANDARDS	SCALE
Workflow Processes Tracking	Roles Meetings Decision-making	How you deliver excellence	What allows the business to grow without chaos

Inside every company, the Owner's Manual Blueprint already exists. Systems, structures, standards, and scale are not abstract business concepts, these are operating in real time every day. Your current role provides direct exposure to how these elements actually work, not how they're described in theory.

Systems show up in the repeatable processes that make work predictable and efficient. Client onboarding, communication flows, invoicing, approvals, delivery timelines. These systems reveal how a business operates from start to finish without constant reinvention. Observing where systems run smoothly and where they break down offers powerful insight into what should be replicated and what should be redesigned later. This is the engine of a business in action.

Structures become visible in how responsibility and authority are organized. Who owns decisions? How are teams arranged? Where does accountability live? Every meeting, handoff, and escalation reveals how structure either supports momentum or creates friction. Understanding structure from the inside shows how clarity, or the lack of it and affects execution. These frameworks shape how work flows and how people collaborate.

Standards reveal themselves in what is tolerated, rewarded, or corrected.

Response times, quality expectations, communication tone, customer experience, and performance metrics all reflect the standards a business operates by. These standards protect reputation and consistency, or quietly erode them. Paying attention here teaches what "good" actually looks like and where lines must be drawn to protect trust.

Scale becomes evident in how the business handles growth. What happens when demand increases? Which systems hold, which crack, and which require reinforcement? Scale is not about effort. It's about infrastructure. Observing how a company grows, hires, automates, and restructures exposes whether growth is sustainable or fragile. There is wisdom in learning these lessons before building anything new.

Studying these four elements from inside a functioning business removes guesswork later. Instead of inventing processes from scratch, patterns are recognized, refined, and reassembled into a future business model built on real-world intelligence rather than trial and error.

Businesses do not need to be built blindly because the workplace is a masterclass in entrepreneurship. Observation with intention is all that's required. Entrepreneurship becomes far less overwhelming after seeing how businesses are built, managed, and sustained. Operational intelligence gathered now prevents years of unnecessary mistakes later. Preparation isn't just about quitting; it's about stepping in ready to lead.

Understanding business infrastructure before launch removes guesswork. Entrepreneurship begins grounded, confident, and equipped to build something that lasts.

Observation alone isn't enough. Insight becomes leverage only when it's captured and organized. As systems, structures, standards, and scale become clear, the next step is intentional transition. This is where loose knowledge becomes portable intelligence. Document what works. Download what belongs to personal capability, not company property. Delegate what must be responsibly transferred before departure. These three actions ensure the exit preserves reputation, relationships, and operational clarity, transforming experience into a foundation that can be carried forward with integrity.

Document everything, because everything matters. This especially applies to the knowledge that lives in someone's head. Remember, it's important to consider any legal implications or restrictions when documenting work. If concerns arise around compliance or intellectual property, seeking professional advice should be part of your Smart Quit planning.

When documenting, focus on processes, templates, best practices, and routines developed over time. Create how-to guides, checklists, or walkthrough videos for workflows others may need to reference after the transition. This supports the team moving forward and contributes to a lasting legacy within the organization. At the same time, maintain a separate, private record of lessons learned, what worked, and what would be done differently. These insights become valuable inputs for the next entrepreneurial chapter, always with legal boundaries clearly respected.

Download anything legally permitted to keep. This may include performance reviews, certifications, portfolios, approved client or vendor contacts, and work samples. Personal records of contributions, such as written reports, designed assets, campaigns, or tools developed should also be collected when allowed. These materials become proof of experience and capability, serving as credibility markers for a future business. Over time, they can be transformed into case studies, testimonials, or other forms of marketing content that demonstrate real-world results.

Lastly, **Delegate.** Delegation isn't just an obligation; it's an act of respect for your role, your team, and the reputation you leave behind. Identify owned responsibilities and determine who is best positioned to take them over. Create a clear transition plans. Whenever possible, train successors. Leave behind stability, not disruption. Done well, delegation allows for an exit on strong terms, preserving relationships, keeping doors open for future collaboration or partnership, and signaling the kind of leader being built in the next chapter.

Smart Quitting isn't about leaving, it's about launching. Taking the time to document expertise, download permitted work product, and delegate responsibilities ensures the transition isn't a retreat from the old, but a step toward the new equipped, prepared, and grounded you.

A clean, confident exit requires preparation well in advance. This work begins now, not the week before your resignation.

The Smart Exit Checklist

Document

☑ Write step-by-step guides for recurring processes you manage

☑ Record screen-share videos explaining complex workflows

☑ Create a folder of SOPs (Standard Operating Procedures) for your role

☑ Make a list of logins, tools, and systems (ensure security compliance)

☑ Note any unwritten rules or insider tips for team members

☑ Document lessons learned, successes, and what you would improve

☑ List all recurring meetings you lead or attend with purposes/agenda

☑ Outline project statuses and next steps for handoff

Download

☑ Save copies of performance reviews, awards, and key emails

☑ Download any portfolios or work samples (only what's ethically and legally yours)

☑ Export your LinkedIn connectors and personal contact lists

☑ Gather testimonials and recommendations from colleagues/clients

☑ Back up your personal email folders (if separate from work email)

☑ Make a copy of training materials or certifications you've completed

☑ Archive any personal notes, ideas, or inspirations stored at work

☑ Export notes or brainstorming sessions relevant to your business

Delegate

☑ List your recurring tasks and assign clear owners

☑ Meet with your manager to review your transition plan

☑ Train or mentor your successor or colleague, if assigned

☑ Set up email out-of-office with forwarding instruction

☑ Clean up your calendar and cancel recurring meetings

☑ Communicate final updates on active projects

☑ Leave behind a written transition plan or FAQ document

☑ Create a 30-day transition timeline
(or whatever time period is appropriate for your position)

SMART QUIT REALITY CHECK

What operational patterns do I see at my current job that work well?

What repeated breakdowns or inefficiencies frustrate me and what do they teach me?

Which systems could I replicate or improve on in my own business?

How do leaders in my company make decisions?
What do I admire or dislike?

What work rhythms, meeting structures, or communication styles do I need to adopt or avoid?

What have I learned about team dynamics that will shape how I hire later?

How does my company handle money, budgeting, or forecasting and what can I learn from it?

What operational insight can I document today that will support my business tomorrow?

Real People. Real Quits. Real Wins.

Robert F. Smith

Smart Quit Age: Late 30s (founded Vista Equity Partners in 2000)
Education: B.S. Chemical Engineering, M.B.A.
Economic Background: Grew up in a middle-class household. Both parents were educators.

Robert F. Smith's entrepreneurial journey is a different kind of Smart Quit™ story, one rooted in mastery, discipline, and the pursuit of solving complex problems at scale. Born in Denver to two educators, Robert grew up in a household that valued excellence, focus, and intellectual curiosity. He was drawn to science early and went on to study chemical engineering at Cornell University. This field sharpened his analytical thinking and obsession with process.

He began his career as an engineer at Goodyear, then Kraft Foods. These roles weren't glamorous, but they were foundational. He learned systems thinking, operational discipline, and process improvement; the very skills that later became the backbone of Vista Equity Partners' investment philosophy.

Ambitious and hungry for broader impact, Robert pursued an MBA at Columbia Business School and transitioned into investment banking at Goldman Sachs. There, he specialized in technology deals, advising companies like Apple, Microsoft, and HP. Robert was not just watching the tech industry grow. He was deeply embedded in its financial architecture.

Yet despite his success, he sensed a persistent gap. Traditional private equity firms didn't understand enterprise software. They undervalued it, mismanaged it, and failed to recognize the recurring revenue power of subscription-based technology.

Robert saw what others didn't. Software wasn't just a product, it was infrastructure.

This insight became the foundation of his Smart Quit™ moment. He didn't leave Goldman Sachs chasing a dream. He left after identifying a precise, overlooked opportunity with billion-dollar potential. He walked away with skill, strategy, and a meticulously built blueprint.

In 2000, he founded Vista Equity Partners, a firm dedicated exclusively to enterprise software, long before SaaS became a mainstream concept. While other firms focused on hardware or consumer goods, Robert committed to a vertical few understood.

Vista developed its own proprietary operating system known as the Vista Standard; a set of repeatable, data-driven best practices used to optimize every company they acquired. This wasn't traditional private equity. It was operational excellence at scale.

The results were unprecedented. Vista consistently produced industry-leading returns and its portfolio companies became category leaders.

Today, Vista manages more than $100 billion in assets, and Robert F. Smith is widely regarded as one of the most successful investors of his generation and is one of the most respected minds in modern finance.

CHAPTER THIRTEEN
NETWORK TO NET WORTH

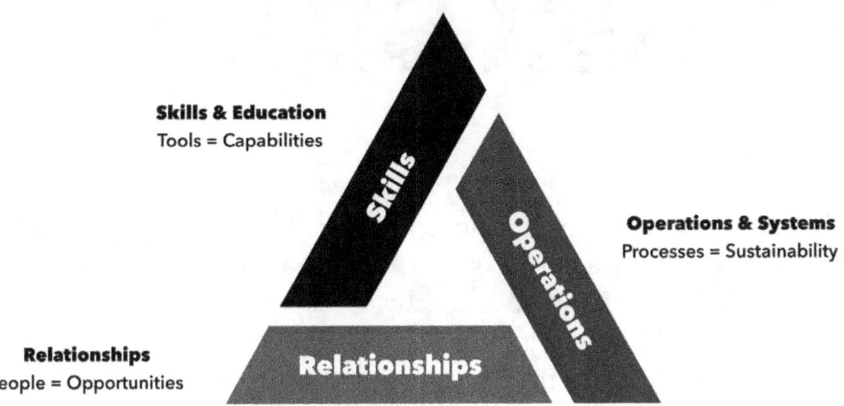

Before a website is built, an LLC is filed, or a product is sold, access already exists to the most powerful accelerator of entrepreneurial success... relationships. A workplace is more than a paycheck, it's where networks, reputations, and future ecosystems are formed. The people working alongside you today may become your first clients, early collaborators, initial referrals, or mentors who guide you in your next chapter. Smart Quitters understand this truth: relationships aren't left behind when a job ends. The value of them moves forward.

Entrepreneurship rewards those who learn to build intentionally early. A job becomes the training ground for connection, influence, contribution, and communication. These skills turn into currency when independence begins. This chapter reveals that relational capital is not accidental; it is strategic, renewable, and essential to building a business that lasts.

The People Power Block™

Most people move through their jobs unaware they're standing inside the first ecosystem of a future business. A workplace is rich with insight, access, and opportunity, if it's handled correctly. Every meeting, hallway conversation, project collaboration, and cross-functional interaction reveals what people struggle with, what they want, and what they would gladly pay to have solved. These aren't just colleagues; they are early indicators of market demand.

When the lens shifts from "coworkers" to "potential collaborators, clients, or referral sources," a job becomes more than a paycheck, it becomes a built-in incubator. Smart Quitters use this season to observe patterns, understand human behavior, and build relational equity long before it's needed.

A company functions as a living focus group. Every inefficiency, complaint, bottleneck, or breakdown contains business insight. The people you work alongside today may become your first customers tomorrow, largely because trust is already established. Professionalism, work ethic, and reliability are visible long before any offer exists. Most early-stage businesses succeed not through polished marketing, but through relationships formed well before any launch.

By paying attention to recurring frustrations, unresolved problems, and missing solutions, early validation begins to form. Smart Quitters observe these pain points quietly and start shaping future value, ethically, strategically, and with clarity.

Among the most important relationships to cultivate are mentors and sponsors. Mentors provide wisdom; sponsors provide access. Both matter. Mentors help refine thinking, offer guidance, and expose blind spots. Sponsors use influence and reputation to open doors. Inside every organization are leaders who have built teams, navigated pressure, and delivered results. These are living previews of the decisions required as an owner or founder.

Smart Quitters intentionally build relationships with people who understand excellence at scale. The goal isn't affirmation, it's acceleration. These relationships often evolve into advisors, connectors, or early credibility when entrepreneurship begins.

Every workplace also holds an untapped pool of talent. These individuals are brilliant but underutilized, entrepreneurial but constrained, loyal but unfulfilled. These may be your future co-founders, early contractors, first employees, or strategic partners. Familiarity with how people work, communicate, and execute becomes a powerful advantage during transition.

Entrepreneurship is not a solo pursuit. Smart Quitters use time inside the workplace to identify complementary skill sets early; operators, analysts, creatives, technologists, project managers, and administrative professionals who keep systems running. Recognizing this talent now prevents reactive hiring later and builds a stronger foundation for what comes next.

Beyond clients and collaborators, the workplace is also where future investors, partners, and strategic stakeholders often originate. Investors rarely back ideas alone; they back people they trust, understand, and have watched perform under pressure. Colleagues, leaders, vendors, and cross-functional partners who have seen execution firsthand already hold data points that matter later. Long before a pitch deck exists, credibility is being built through consistency, integrity, and results. These relationships often become the warm introductions that open funding conversations, partnership opportunities, or strategic support when the time is right.

Partnerships and resource access follow the same principle. Distribution partners, vendors, advisors, legal support, financial professionals, and industry connectors are frequently encountered inside existing professional environments. Observing how these relationships function, who holds influence, how decisions are made, and where value is exchanged creates a map for future collaboration. Smart Quitters pay attention to who controls resources, who accelerates outcomes, and who moves opportunity forward. When relationships are built early, entrepreneurship doesn't begin from scarcity; it begins with access.

Network Mining Map™: Extracting value from your current workplace

The first step to extracting value from the relationships in your workplace is mapping the relational ecosystem long before leaving. Relationship mapping is the intentional process of identifying who inspires you, who challenges you, who opens doors, who knows your industry best, and who can amplify your message. It's about clarity, not convenience.

By mapping peers, leaders, vendors, alumni, and clients, a relational runway begins to take shape. This is the support that lasts well beyond any resignation letter. This map could evolve into a referral network, an advisory board, a community, or be your early customer base. Planning here reduces pressure later.

With a network map in place, the focus shifts to becoming a magnet and building an internal brand. Your internal brand is your reputation and the story that is told about you when you're not in the room. Even before launching a business, your internal brand follows you into the next chapter. Excellence, ownership, communication, and integrity convert colleagues into future clients and champions. People buy into credibility long before they buy any product.

This is never about working harder; it's about showing up consistently at a high level. Trust in work, respect for judgment, and visible impact turn colleagues into ambassadors for future ventures even without ever asking. That's the power of relational equity and a cultivated internal brand.

Relationships are assets only when maintained. Leadership expert John Maxwell puts it simply: win the heart before asking for the hand. Smart Quitters nurture connections with intention, not manipulation. Connections aren't collected, they're nurtured. Staying in touch, offering value, being supportive, and showing up authentically are the habits that make your network durable and valuable.

The Four C's of Relationship Leverage

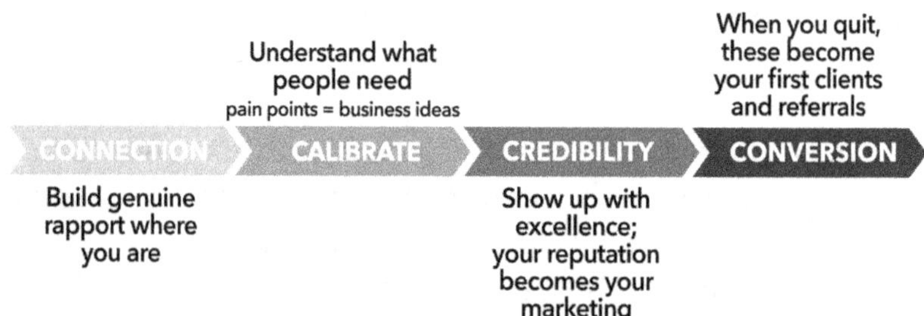

Building a strong network isn't about collecting contacts, it's about creating relational equity that fuels your future business. Smart Quitters understand that relationships are assets, and that investing in them now will pay dividends later. Here's our recap in Four C's:

Connection
Identify the people who inspire, challenge, open doors, and amplify your work. These aren't just coworkers. They are mentors, sponsors, collaborators, future clients, and potential partners. Strategic connections become the backbone of your entrepreneurial ecosystem.

Calibrate
The skill of reading people and situations with enough precision that relationships compound into future opportunity. It means noticing how someone thinks, what they value, what pressures they're under, and what "success" looks like for them, then matching timing, tone, and follow-up accordingly. This creates trust and relevance, which is what turns a connection into a future referral, partnership, client, or open door. Over time, calibration builds relationship leverage: a network that supports your next business move because the relationship was built intentionally long before anything was needed.

Credibility
Build trust and authority before you ever launch. Excellence, reliability, and consistent contribution inside your current role create a reputation that travels with you. When people already respect your work, they are more

likely to support your next venture.

Conversion
Turn relational equity into action. Mentors advise, sponsors open doors, collaborators partner, and early colleagues become clients or advocates. Observing, learning, and contributing now allows for seamless integration of these relationships into your entrepreneurial journey.

Relational equity is intentional, renewable, and measurable. Smart Quitters are constantly building their network and treat every meeting, project, and hallway conversation as an opportunity to strengthen connections, clarify value, and build credibility.

When the time comes to step into entrepreneurship, these relationships are no longer theoretical, they are real assets that accelerate growth, reduce risk, and open doors. Every connection cultivated, every insight gained, and every ounce of trust earned becomes fuel for the next chapter.

In the end, relational equity transforms the workplace from a paycheck into a propellant. By focusing on connections, clarity, credibility, and conversion, Smart Quitters ensure that when they leave, they're not just starting a business, they're stepping into a network already primed for success.

You are never just leaving people behind. You are expanding the context of how you relate to them. Treat every relationship like a seed that's watered over time. It becomes opportunities you couldn't have manufactured later. This is how Smart Quitters turn a job into an ecosystem.

Relationships aren't a "nice-to-have" on your Smart Quit journey, they are your greatest multiplier. The people in your life determine the rooms you enter, the opportunities that find you, and the momentum you carry into entrepreneurship. When you leverage relationships well, you don't start your business alone, you start it with a community already rooting for you.

You have no idea which connection will change your future. That's why you treat every relationship with intention today. Your network isn't just behind you, it's beside you. And in your next chapter, it will grow ahead of you.

SMART QUIT REALITY CHECK

Who in my current workplace has already influenced my growth? How and why?

What types of people do I naturally connect with? Where might I need to stretch myself?

Which relationships feel like seeds (connections that could grow into something meaningful later)?

Where have I undervalued my internal brand, and how can I strengthen it?

Who could become a mentor or sponsor for my next chapter?

Which colleagues or industry contacts show signs of being future collaborators or clients?

How well do the people around me understand what I'm capable of?

What's one relationship I can invest in more intentionally this week?

Real People. Real Quits. Real Wins.

Leila Janah

Smart Quit Age: ~28 (founded Samasource in 2008; born Oct. 9, 1982).
Education: B.A., African Development Studies
Economic Background: Child of Indian immigrants who experienced financial difficulties

Leila Janah's Smart Quit™ story wasn't about escaping a job. It was about refusing to accept a world where talent is evenly distributed, but opportunity isn't. She didn't just find her passion. She found a problem so clear that it demanded a solution.

Early in her career, Leila saw how many people in low-income communities had intelligence, drive, and potential but no access to stable, dignified work. She also saw that businesses everywhere were outsourcing digital work, spending millions on tasks that could be done from anywhere. The gap wasn't capability. The gap was connection.

That insight became her breakthrough. Instead of waiting for the system to change, Leila built a new system.

She founded Samasource with a simple but powerful model: deliver high-quality digital services to major companies while creating fair-wage work for people who had been shut out of the economy. It wasn't charity. It was business, anchored in impact. She took a problem most people talk about and turned it into infrastructure.

Leila didn't start with a massive budget or a polished platform. She started with clarity. She built partnerships, earned trust, and created a repeatable operating model that proved two things at once: companies would pay for excellent work, and underrepresented talent could deliver it when given the opportunity and tools.

Her Smart Quit™ move wasn't dramatic. It was strategic. She chose mission and margins. She chose a model that could scale. She didn't chase attention, she chased outcomes.

The lesson in her story is one every employee considering entrepreneurship needs to hear: the advantage isn't about having the perfect conditions. The advantage is seeing what others ignore and building something practical enough to work in the real world. Leila didn't wait to be invited into the future. She built a bridge and then created a pathway for others to cross it.

In the middle of difficulty lies opportunity.
Albert Einstein

CHAPTER FOURTEEN
FREEDOM ISN'T FREE

Most aspiring entrepreneurs don't fail from lack of talent. They fail because they leap without a landing. They leave too soon, guided by emotion, assuming passion alone will carry them.

But passion without structure quickly becomes panic. We are not accepting panic entrepreneurship. A Smart Quit is planned, well-resourced, fully embodied entrepreneurship. This chapter shows how to protect your mind, money, momentum, and peace while making the transition.

A financial runway isn't "extra savings." It's a freedom cushion that lets you:

> Say "no" to misaligned clients who drain energy

> Say "yes" to opportunities that need patience to mature

> Grow with clarity instead of desperation

> Build with confidence instead of fear

Money doesn't buy happiness but it does buy time to make aligned decisions. Time is the real luxury. Time is the real power. Time is the real freedom. Money is how that freedom is created.

Calculate your Real-Life Number. This is not a stripped-down, bare-bones budget. Entrepreneurship shouldn't shrink life; it should design a sustainable, dignified lifestyle runway that supports your business and the life you actually want.

Step 1: Identify Your True Monthly Cost of Living

List the following:

> Housing
>
> Utilities
>
> Groceries
>
> Transportation
>
> Insurance
>
> Children's needs
>
> Debt payments
>
> Medical needs
>
> Non-negotiable life maintaining expenses

This is your stability baseline.

Step 2 : Add Your Emotional Cost of Living

These are the things that keep you feeling human, not depleted:

> Beauty/grooming rituals
>
> Gym or wellness membership
>
> Therapy or coaching
>
> Weekly leisure or joy moment

This is your well-being baseline. Add it in.

Your Life Number equals:

Cost of Living Baseline
+ Well-Being Baseline
= Your Monthly Life Number

This is the number that protects your peace, your dignity, your health, and your ability to show up. Not minimal survival, but sustainable expansion.

Determining Your Financial Runway

RUNWAY *RISK TOLERANCE*	WHO'S IT FOR	OUTCOME
6 Months *High*	Already has savings, sales and/or demand	Quicker launch, builds on momentum
9 Months *Mid*	Steady momentum in side hustle/startup Lower bridge number	Safe, steady, low-stress transition Allows focus
12 Months *Low*	Has dependents High debt Longer transition	Deep peace, very stable launch

A financial runway measures how many months life and business can be sustained without relying on a paycheck. Typical ranges are 6, 9, or 12 months. The right choice depends on current financial positioning, the stage of a side hustle or startup, and risk tolerance.

12 months: for risk-averse individuals or those with significant financial responsibilities; provides stability and breathing room.

9 months: for moderate risk tolerance; offers balance between safety and momentum.

6 months: for high risk tolerance, existing revenue, or the ability to pivot quickly.

The goal is a runway that aligns with comfort and capacity to build, ensuring a confident exit rather than a reckless leap.

Discover a personal financial runway. There is no universally "right" answer, only the truth of the life being built.

The Bridge Income Strategy
Most books skip this part, but it's critical. The goal isn't to replace an entire salary before quitting. The goal is to create enough consistent cash flow to extend your runway, reduce pressure, and give the business space to grow properly.

Bridge income is temporary revenue generated during the transition from employment to entrepreneurship. Think of it as the financial cushion that shortens the gap between quitting and reaching full profitability.

Bridge income should match risk tolerance. Lower tolerance means replacing a higher percentage of the monthly life number before leaving a job, creating stability and confidence while the business grows.

Bridge Income Target should be 60 -80% of your Monthly Life Number
This is your first business milestone.
Not $10K per month.
Not six figures.
Not launch hype.
Bridge Income = calm, strategic, grounded growth.

Building your financial runway and bridge income starts with knowing exactly how much you need and then creating the plan to accumulate it. This isn't about saving blindly. It's about structuring your money so you can sustain your life and fund your transition. This is accomplished through a mix of reducing expenses, increasing income, reallocating resources, and creating temporary revenue streams that support your exit. Once you understand the total number you're aiming for, you can use runway stacking methods to accelerate how quickly you reach it and create a cushion that matches your risk tolerance and goals.

Runway Stacking Methods

Save: Automatic transfers. Non-negotiable. No emotional decisions.

Reduce: Not deprivation. Redirection. Where are you spending to cope with the job you're leaving? What if that energy and resources was going toward your exit?

Replace: Start a Bridge Offer now. One client at a time. One product batch at a time. One sale at a time.

Redirect: Bonuses, tax returns, side checks go straight to your runway, not lifestyle inflation. This is exit fuel.

EXAMPLES

The Analyst
Salary: $98,000
Monthly life number: $6,800
Bridge income goal: $5,500/month
Offer: Strategy sessions + light execution support
Runway built through: Expense reduction, early client retainers, and stacking part-time consulting projects
Quit after: 7 months

Scaled to: A full client roster, premium strategy retainers, and a stream-lined 4-day workweek
Quit: Calm. Grounded. Planned.

The Product Maker
Salary: $62,000
Monthly life number: $4,900
Bridge income goal: $3,200/month
Offer: Lifestyle products + small batch physical goods
Runway built through: Preorders, small batch drops, audience warm-ups, and consistent demand testing
Quit after: 9 months
Scaled to: A recognizable lifestyle brand, repeat buyers, and expanded product lines
Quit: Steady. Strategic. Demand-driven.

The Fractional COO
Salary: $128,000
Monthly life number: $7,400
Bridge income goal: $4,000/month
Offer: Fractional operations + team management support
Runway built through: Staying employed while building a consulting roster, stacking 90-day projects, and securing early anchor clients
Quit after: 8 months
Scaled to: A multi-client consulting practice, waitlisted capacity, and higher-ticket operational leadership packages
Quit: Validated. Systematic. Sustainable.

Every one of them left without panic, without debt spirals and without self-betrayal. This is the Smart Quit.

Your transition has now moved from:

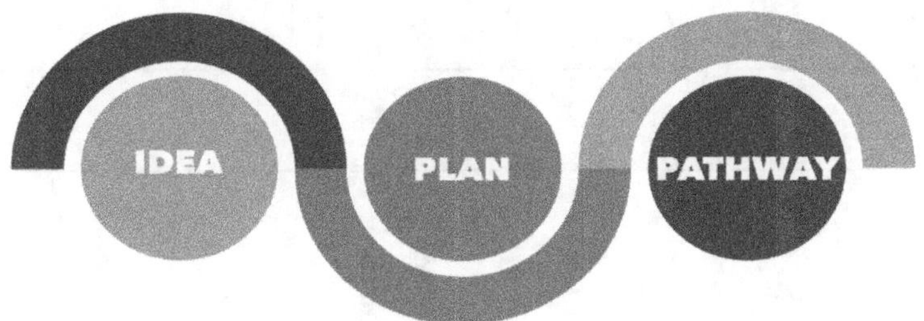

Money changes your options.
Identity changes your execution.
This is where you win.

SMART QUIT REALITY CHECK

136

My Monthly Life Number is: $ ______________________

My Chosen Runway Length: 6 mo   9 mo   12 mo

My Runway Goal: $ ______________________

My Bridge Income Goal: $ ______________________ per month

The Simplest Offer I can use to reach my Bridge Income is:

____

____

____

Real People. Real Quits. Real Wins.

Arlan Hamilton

Smart Quit Age: 34 years old (founded Backstage Capital in 2015)
Education: No formal college degree; self-taught entrepreneur and investor
Economic Background: Raised in a low-income, single-parent household

When Arlan Hamilton, began Backstage Capital, she was told as a gay Black woman with no college degree or tech background that she didn't "fit" the startup model. She became homeless, sleeping on airport floors while trying to break into venture capital. Arlan Hamilton didn't have a safety net, a degree, or a clear path when she decided to rewrite her story. She was in her mid-thirties and broke, but she had a vision that wouldn't let her go: to build a venture capital firm that invested in founders who looked like her.

Before her entrepreneurial leap, Arlan had spent years working in the music industry managing tours and logistics for artists, but she was frustrated watching a world where money and opportunity flowed almost exclusively to white, male founders. She realized she didn't just want to work in someone else's business, she wanted to change the system entirely.
With no connections and no capital, she began teaching herself about startups and investing, building a network from scratch. Armed with her laptop and a belief that underrepresented founders were being overlooked, she started writing her business plan.

In 2015, she founded Backstage Capital, a venture firm built to fund women, people of color, and LGBTQ+ founders who had been overlooked by traditional investors. At first, Arlan thought success meant becoming one of the big players in Venture Capital, launching billion-dollar funds, being featured in Forbes, and scaling fast. But after years of relentless pushing, she found herself burned out, under pressure to perform as a "savior" for all underrepresented founders and constantly defending her methods. She made the decision to redefine success as protecting her peace and health, funding without compromising her values and lastly, measuring success by impact and not just capital raised. She had to stop trying to be everyone's hero and start being her own.

During her entrepreneurial journey Arlan had to deal with impostor syndrome and being the "only one in the room", the emotional toll of constantly justifying her vision to skeptical investors, the public pressure to succeed on behalf of an entire movement and the struggle to set boundaries and say no even after achieving success. Despite the noise, she stayed grounded in her mission because she knew her focus was not being liked, but creating change.

Arlan redefined success not by assimilation, but by disruption. She didn't get a seat at the table, so she built her own table and funded over 200 startups lead by underrepresented founders in the process. Her journey proves not only that the traditional entrepreneurial path is not the only path, but the mission can be more powerful than pedigree and you don't need permission to bet on yourself or on others to like you.

Backstage Capital's commitment to diversity and inclusion in the venture capital space has not only provided capital to underrepresented founders, but has also challenged the traditional norms of the industry paving the way for a more equitable entrepreneurial ecosystem.

Since its inception, Backstage Capital has invested in more than 200 startups, raised millions in funding, and reshaped the narrative around what success and access can look like in venture capital.

Arlan's story isn't about walking away from a job, it's about walking toward justice, ownership, and impact. She didn't just quit. She built the stage she'd been waiting to stand on.

CHAPTER FIFTEEN
THE QUIET SMART QUIT

There are usually red flags and green lights signaling when it's time to move on. Many wait for the "perfect moment," but in reality, that moment rarely exists. The signs are what matter. They are sometimes subtle, sometimes loud but the message is clear: it's time to take action.

Signs can be external. A diminishing sense of value, a shrinking role, changes in company stability or leadership, or a vision and direction that no longer align with personal values. They can also be internal: a growing pull toward entrepreneurial dreams, an idea that won't leave the mind, or a desire for greater control over time, impact, and income. Observing both internal and external signals is the first step toward reclaiming agency and shaping your next chapter.

A Smart Quit is not emotional or impulsive. It is strategic, intentional, informed, and well-planned. It's not about storming out in frustration, but about pausing to assess financial runway, support systems, and the skills and experience available before taking the leap.

The goal isn't to see your Smart Quit as an escape, but as a transition into something aligned with purpose, potential, and passion. The tension between your current work and who you truly can be is a clear signal that preparation is needed. This isn't rebellion, it's a declaration of a new vision.

There's no need to make a scene to make a move. Remaining under the radar while building the next chapter is strategic, not dishonest. It preserves energy for what matters most. Trust your instincts, plan intentionally, and remember: the courage to step away is often the first step toward building the life and career that fits what you truly want.

Signs You're Ready to Smart Quit with Purpose:

Meeting expectations, but no longer chasing promotions

No longer tying identity to a job title

Mentally clocking out to focus on a bigger mission

Constantly daydreaming about your entrepreneurial journey

Craving autonomy and creative control

Ready to trade security for fulfillment

Building on the side and but now ready to step into the light

Values no longer align with your company's

Already operating like a founder

Protecting your peace may require emotional detachment from your role or company. The biggest cost isn't time, it's energy. If the job drains the soul, nothing is left to build the future. Accept walking away from recognition that no longer serves your growth or purpose.

The 3 Ps of Emotional Detachment

Perspective
This job is a tool, not a measure of self-worth.

Protection
Say no. Take PTO. Skip the happy hour. Be strategic with time and treat it as the most valuable resource.

Priorities
Not everything is an emergency.

Mastering the 3 Ps; prioritizing, gaining perspective, and protecting peace, creates a space to operate from direction rather than reaction. Emotional detachment alone isn't enough to advance. The next step is moving from managing everything mentally to building systems that support the transition. This framework organizes work, lightens the load, and frees the operational and mental bandwidth needed to create what comes next.

When you emotionally detach and prepare for your exit, you are not just preparing to leave something behind. You are becoming a new version of yourself. The foundation being laid now is the catalyst for everything yet to be built.

Real People. Real Quits. Real Wins.

Justin Welsh

Smart Quit Age: 35 years old (Started The Saturday Solopreneur in 2019)
Education: B.S. in Business Administration
Economic Background: Middle-class; raised by hardworking parents who valued independence and resilience.

Justin Welsh is a former SaaS senior executive who helped several companies scale to over $50M+ in revenue. He lived the traditional hustle life of an employee, including long hours, constant pressure and high performance. Despite what most saw from the outside as a successful career, Justin experienced intense burnout and anxiety. He eventually walked away from his job with no other employment lined up, no plan (no he did not Smart Quit), but with a clear decision that he would not allow what the world saw as success cost him his peace and health.

He launched a multi-million dollar business which offers digital products, newsletters and an online community on LinkedIn growth and soloprenership. He had zero employees and no investor meetings. Finally, he stopped building someone else's dream and built a calm business around his own life, instead of running someone else's stressful business. He began prioritizing his life over his work. This did not come without it's own challenges as he battled the loneliness and identity crisis that came with leaving the "important" titles of his job behind.

However, Justin was able to achieve remarkable success as a solopreneur, building his multi-million dollar business, with a 90% profit margin, all without employees or paid advertising. He defined his value system for what he wanted out of his entrepreneurial life, put boundaries in place and found massive success within it.

CHAPTER SIXTEEN
EXIT SMART. EXIT STEADY. EXIT READY.

A Smart Quit is not a dramatic exit at 2:17 PM on a random Tuesday. It is quiet, structured, intentional, strategic, and deeply self-respecting. Departing in this way protects relationships, preserves reputation, and safeguards peace. Done correctly, a Smart Quit can even position one for future referrals, partnerships, or return opportunities. Leaving a job in this manner is not an escape, it's a deliberate transition to the next level.

The exit is executed like a CEO, not a runaway intern. The goal is to leave no mess, no confusion, no burned bridges, and no unnecessary emotional fallout. Closure is left behind for the team, clarity for the organization, and confidence for what comes next. This approach reflects maturity, professionalism, and leadership.

Exiting begins long before any resignation is submitted. First, identity shifts; next, the calendar and priorities; then, the role itself; and lastly, the job.

Execution Guidelines:

Shifting responsibility, not abandoning it: Identify ownership, determine what must be handed off, and ensure successors are prepared.

Documenting critical knowledge: Create standard operating procedures, walkthrough notes, and key contact lists. This isn't for the company; it's for a clean exit and personal integrity.

Removing emotional entanglement: Leave without venting, gossiping, dramatic reveals, or foreshadowing departure. Peace is maintained through privacy and deliberate preparation.

The Four Phases of the Smart Quit Exit

PHASE 1: Internal Decision (The Silent Stage)
The decision is made, quietly. No announcements. No leaks. Focus stays on building the financial runway and bridge income while operating with discipline and discretion.

PHASE 2: Transition Preparation
Preparation begins behind the scenes. Responsibilities are gradually delegated. Knowledge is documented. Nonessential meetings are reduced. Emotional attachment to the role is intentionally loosened. The exit is being built long before it's spoken.

PHASE 3: The Conversation
A direct, calm, professional meeting is scheduled. No theatrics. No over-explaining. Just clarity.

Be prepared to say something like:

"I've appreciated my time here and I'm grateful for the opportunities I've had. I've decided to transition into a new chapter, and I want to ensure the handoff is clean and supportive. My proposed last day is [date]. I've outlined a transition plan to make this as smooth as possible."

This isn't a request. It's an informed decision, delivered with respect. More on this in the next chapter.

PHASE 4: The Handoff
Execute the transition plan.
Train where needed.
Close loops.
Walk away clean.

What Not to Do:

Do not explain your dream.

Do not overshare the plan.

Do not seek validation.

Do not guilt or second-guess your decision.

Do not negotiate with destiny.

Do not get tempted by more money or a better title.

Do not seek permission.

The timeline for each phase will vary based on several factors: role scope, financial runway, and the strength and maturity of the business being built. For some, a Smart Quit is a five-month plan. For others, it's a five-year strategy. In many cases, an employer may be funding education, certifications, or leadership development, and those benefits become part of the exit strategy, not a delay, but leverage.

And remember: a plan is a guide, not a guarantee. Life doesn't always honor timelines. When a six-month exit plan was once presented to an employer, the response was gracious and final, three days later.

So yes, plan for the best.
And prepare for the unexpected.

Here's the emotional truth. There will likely be sadness, because a familiar identity is being released. There may be fear, because the next level always demands more. But there is often relief too-because the internal shift has already happened. The soul usually moves first. All of this is normal. It's human.

Freedom isn't the absence of fear.
Freedom is moving forward with fear and choosing self-trust anyway.

That's it.
That's growth.

SMART QUIT REALITY CHECK

When I picture myself leaving my current job, what's the worst-case story I'm telling myself and how much of it is fact vs. fear?

What am I actually afraid of losing: money, identity, stability, status, relationships, or certainty?

If I stay, what will it cost me; time, health, confidence, peace, or momentum?

What's on the other side that's worth the risk: more freedom, more income, more impact, more time, or more alignment?

What's my first smart step toward it?

Real People. Real Quits. Real Wins.

Tristan Walker

Smart Quit Age: 29 years old (Founded Walker & Company Brands in 2013)
Education: B.A. in Economics, MBA
Economic Background: Grew up in a low-income household. Raised by his mother after his father passed away when he was young.

Tristan Walker's story is a masterclass in culturally intelligent entrepreneurship, intentional timing, and quitting with clarity, not emotion. After business school, he entered the heart of Silicon Valley at a time when very few black founders were given oxygen, visibility, or investment.

He built a career marked by rapid learning and strategic positioning, interning at Twitter and later joining the early team at Foursquare, where he ran business development and was responsible for forging partnerships that helped the company scale during its peak growth years. Tristan was ascending quickly, earning credibility inside an industry that often questioned whether someone with his background "fit the mold."

Yet behind the accolades was a deeper misalignment. He didn't see Silicon Valley building solutions for people who looked like him. The tools, products, and platforms being created had global reach but rarely accounted for diverse lived experiences. Tristan recognized that he could continue climbing the tech ladder or he could step into a purpose that demanded more of him.

His Smart Quit™ moment.

He didn't quit because he couldn't succeed. He quit because he saw a gap that no one else was willing or equipped to solve. That gap was grooming for black men. For decades, razors and shaving systems had been engineered for straight hair textures, not for the curly hair that leads to ingrown hairs, razor bumps, and skin irritation. It was a problem Black men simply lived with, not because it couldn't be solved, but because no one bothered to solve it. Tristan set out to change that with Bevel, a single-blade razor system designed specifically for coarse, curly hair.

His MVP was stunningly simple: a razor, a brush, and skin-prep product built from real dermatological research and cultural understanding. It wasn't flashy. It wasn't broad. It was precise. And it resonated immediately.

Bevel wasn't just a product; it was a reclamation of dignity in an overlooked category. The brand's identity was clean, masculine, intentional, and modern; an aesthetic that reflected the future of Black luxury. Demand was validated quickly. Customers didn't just buy the razor; they became loyalists because it solved a problem they'd dealt with for years.

As Bevel grew, Tristan expanded the vision to form Walker & Company Brands, a platform dedicated to creating health and beauty products for people of color globally. He built a team grounded in cultural fluency, operational rigor, and the belief that communities deserve products designed with them in mind, not as an afterthought.

In 2018, Walker & Company was acquired by Procter & Gamble, making Tristan one of the first Black founders to sell a company to the world's largest consumer goods corporation. He later became the first Black CEO of a P&G subsidiary, proof that when you build with clarity, precision, and cultural truth, even the biggest institutions must evolve.

Dream big, start small, but most of all, start.
Simon Sinek

CHAPTER SEVENTEEN
WRITING YOUR EXIT STORY

Most people assume quitting a job is as simple as handing HR a letter and saying, "I'm done." Smart Quitters understand it's far more nuanced. A resignation letter is not a formality; it is a snapshot of legacy, professionalism, and the bridge into the next chapter. Done well, it positions the exit as confident, competent, and credible. Done poorly, it creates unnecessary friction, damaged relationships, and lingering regret.

A resignation functions as a pathway. On one side stands the current role; on the other, the entrepreneurial future. The letter becomes the structure that allows a clean crossing-leaving clarity behind and stepping forward prepared. This is not merely a two-week notice; it is a declaration of independence. The way separation is communicated shapes how the departure is remembered. Tone, clarity, and restraint matter. Messaging should reflect intention, maturity, and thoughtful decision-making.

Principles for a graceful exit:

> Keep communication short, clear, and neutral
> Express gratitude, even when the chapter is closing with relief
> Focus forward rather than revisiting what went wrong

Perception carries weight, especially in close industries. How an exit is handled often matters as much as why it happens. A poorly managed departure can raise doubts about judgment and character, not just competence and re-building trust takes time, consistency, and new proof points.

Send a final "farewell" email to select colleagues, highlighting your new path without pitching.

PLANT THE SEED.

Even when a role was draining or misaligned, there is no advantage in scorched-earth exits. Observers are always present, and today's colleagues can become tomorrow's partners, clients, or advocates.

The goal is to build bridges, not burn them. When appropriate and strategic, extended notice can reinforce professionalism. Documentation should already be complete-processes, procedures, and key knowledge transferred. Support during the transition can be offered within reasonable bounds, while remembering that final responsibility does not belong to the departing role.

It may seem like "just a letter," but it carries weight:

It becomes part of an official record

It shapes narrative and perception

It reduces risk by keeping emotion out of documentation

It signals a next-level identity: prepared, professional, and intentional

Emotion stays private. Strategy stays visible. What remains is respect, not resentment and a clean foundation for what comes next.

The Anatomy of a Smart Quit Resignation Letter

A resignation letter isn't a manifesto. It's a strategic communication tool.

Here's what to include:

1. Clear statement of resignation
Example: "I am writing to formally resign from my position as Marketing Manager at XYZ Company."

2. Effective date / last working day
Example: "My last day will be March 15, 2026."

3. Professional + neutral tone
Avoid venting, oversharing, or making excuses.

4. Gratitude statement
Example: "I appreciate the opportunities to grow professionally and collaborate with such a talented team."

5. Transition support
Example: "I will document processes, complete outstanding projects, and assist in training a replacement during my notice period."

Optional add-ons:
30-day transition plan
Offer for limited post-exit support
Notes on delegated responsibilities
Remember, less is more. A resignation letter is documentation, not a confession.

Every situation calls for a different tone. Choose the one that fits your context.

Smart Quit Exit Styles

TONE	WHEN TO USE	CHARACTERISTICS
Simple & Direct	Neutral Relationships	Short, professional, minimal
Warm & Grateful	Want future referrals	Personal, appreciative
Boundary-Focused	Toxic Environments	Clean, neutral, final
Executive/Strategic	Turning role into an opportunity	Includes transition plan, optional future support

A resignation letter is the story of an exit, told with intention.

What to avoid:
- Venting about management or coworkers
- Long explanations or justifications
- Emotional ultimatums or dramatic language

How to reframe:
- "This transition supports my long-term goals and future direction."
- "A decision has been made for me to pursue a role aligned with a deeper focus on a skill, passion, or growth."

The story belongs to you. Tell it once. Tell it clearly. And when possible, leave the door open.

Sample Resignation Letters

Professional & Direct

I am writing to formally resign from my position as [Title] at [Company Name], effective [Date]. I appreciate the experience I've gained and will support a smooth transition over the notice period.

Warm & Grateful

I'm submitting my resignation from [Title], with my final day on [Date]. I am grateful for the opportunities to grow, the relationships I've built, and the lessons learned. I will document processes and assist in training a replacement to ensure a seamless handoff.

Minimal / Boundary-Focused

Please accept this as formal notice of my resignation from [Company Name], effective [Date]. I will transition my responsibilities professionally during this period.

Strategic / Phased Transition

I am resigning from my role as [Title], effective [Date]. Over the next 30 days, I will document key processes, hand off projects, and train team members as needed. I am also available for limited support post-transition, if helpful.

Sometimes the conversation happens before a formal resignation letter is submitted. In those moments, brevity and composure matter.

If working with a supportive manager:
"I've decided to pursue a new direction aligned with long-term goals. The priority is making this transition smooth and professional."

If working with a challenging manager or in a toxic environment:
"This is formal notice of resignation, effective [date]. Responsibilities will be transitioned professionally."

For a team announcement:
"I wanted to share that I'm moving on from my role at [Company Name]. A great deal was learned here, and support for a smooth transition will continue over the next [X weeks]."

Final Checklist Before Sending

- ☑ Clear final day stated

- ☑ Professional, neutral tone

- ☑ Gratitude expressed where appropriate

- ☑ Transition plan included if needed

Read it aloud. Does it sound grounded, composed, and intentional, not reactive or resentful?

A Smart Quit is deliberate. This is not closure for your boss; it is the launch of the next chapter with control.

A resignation letter is more than a notice document. It is a strategic signal of your new identity. It protects reputation, preserves relationships, and establishes credibility while you step into entrepreneurship. This move is not a blind leap. It is a calculated, confident step forward.

Letting go carries emotion. Excitement, fear, relief, and nausea can coexist all in the same hour. That's normal. An old identity is being shed and that's a little scary.

The 72-Hour Rule:
Allow three days without filling the space. No announcements. No posts. Let the nervous system catch up with the decision.

Exit Plan Recap

- ☑ Leverage people who accelerate opportunity and open doors

- ☑ Use tools that expand capability, credibility, and competence

- ☑ Apply systems and processes that create stability, scalability, and sustainability

- ☑ Document, Download, Delegate

- ☑ Set successors up for success and protect the brand

- ☑ Craft a clear resignation narrative

- ☑ Stay connected without burning bridges

- ☑ Honor the return on investment received from the employer

A job is not the enemy; it is an investor. It funds growth, underwrite skill development, and bankroll a future business without taking equity. When a mindset can shift from frustration to strategy, every paycheck, project, and meeting reveals its preparation value.

Do not burn the bridge, build on it. Leaving with intention, not resentment, is how a Smart Quit happens. Like a founder. Not a fugitive.

SMART QUIT REALITY CHECK

Write one sentence describing your next chapter, keep it positive, strategic, and forward-looking.

Draft your resignation letter using one of the provided templates as a guide.

Circle the tone that aligns with your exit:
Direct / Grateful / Boundary-Focused / Strategic

Create your 30-day transition checklist.

Write your "one-sentence next chapter statement" for framing in your resignation letter.

Real People. Real Quits. Real Wins.

Andy Dunn

Smart Quit Age: 28 years old (co-founded Bonobos in 2007)
Education: B.A. in Economics; M.B.A.
Economic Background: Middle-class upbringing in Chicago; mother was an artist and author, father an entrepreneur in manufacturing

Andy Dunn is best known as the co-founder and former CEO of Bonobos, the men's apparel company that revolutionized e-commerce with a focus on fit and customer service. Prior to Bonobos, Dunn was a consultant at Bain & Company where he honed his analytical and business strategy skills. Dunn's move from employee to CEO required major internal and external behavioral changes. "When you're an employee, you can always point to a boss, or a process, or a system. When you're the CEO, there's no one else to blame"... but you.

When you are the boss you own every outcome. As a consultant, Dunn had the freedom to work in frameworks. As a founder he had to act on incomplete data, make hard calls quickly and take emotional and financial risks daily. In Dunn's experience there was a shift where emotional intelligence mattered more than raw intelligence. Early in his transition he struggled with managing relationships, tension and team dynamics and had to learn not only how to hire, but also how to inspire, resolve conflict and to set culture.

As there's a recent focus on the vulnerability of the mental health of entrepreneurs and CEOs, many leaders can be heard talking about how "lonely it is at the top". In Dunn's memoir, Burn Rate: launching a Startup and Losing My Mind, he shares about being the founder, the firestarter, but also the arsonist at Bonobos and how his story is a cautionary tale about ignoring inner well being in the name of outer success. He described his experience with bipolar disorder and how the high-energy traits of his manic episodes fueled rapid company growth (the "fire") while also creating crises (the "arson").

In 2017, Walmart acquired Bonobos for $310 million in a controversial deal that some feared would dilute the brand, but marked a major win for the DTC (direct to consumer) movement and validated Bonobos as a serious player.

Dunn's story is about more than building a brand, it's about personal transformation and emotional intelligence in leadership, a true mindset shift. After stepping down, Dunn publicly shared his experience with bipolar disorder and mental health, using his platform to destigmatize vulnerability in business. He highlights the emotional cost of entrepreneurship and a call for a new kind of founder: one who leads with both courage and compassion.

Stage Three:
PIVOT

Success is knowing your purpose in life, growing to reach your maximum potential, and sowing seeds that benefit others.
John Maxwell

CHAPTER EIGHTEEN
LEVEL UP

The hardest part of leaving a job isn't the resignation conversation, the logistics, the timing, or even the financial planning. The hardest part is unlearning who you had to become to succeed while working for someone else.

That identity that made you valuable as an employee is not the same identity that will make you powerful as a founder.

You were trained to keep the peace.
Be agreeable.
Be reliable.
Wait your turn.
Seek approval.
Follow structure.
Perform for evaluation.
To route decisions through someone else.

Entrepreneurship demands the opposite. It requires;
Leading without permission.
Trusting your own judgment.
Choosing proactively.

Moving before validation.
Owning outcomes.
Building structure instead of waiting for it.
Creating value instead of proving worth.

Entrepreneurship isn't just a career shift.
It's a self-concept shift.

A business cannot be built from an approval-based identity, a dependence on validation, or a habit of performing for praise. Leadership collapses when confidence still needs external confirmation.

Becoming a CEO means trusting your voice, your choices, and your timing, often without applause or reassurance. That stretch is the work.

The employee-to-CEO transition is difficult because years were spent being rewarded for making yourself smaller to keep things running smoothly. Being dependable. Being the one who always figured it out. Carrying responsibility quietly. Holding everything together.

EMPLOYEE ENERGY	CEO ENERGY
"Tell me what to do."	"I decide what happens next."
Performs to meet expectations	Operates from personal standards
Waits for instructions, clarity, approval	Creates clarity, structure, direction
Avoids mistakes	Knows mistakes = growth data
Values being liked	Values being respected
Work = identity	Work = one expression of identity

Those traits are celebrated in the workplace. They're also the traits that quietly drain you as an entrepreneur when misaligned.

An identity can become tied to responsibility, reliability, excellence, and competence. These are beautiful qualities that, when overused, create resentment. This is not because of failure, but because a person can become indispensable to everyone except themselves.

Now it's time to reverse that.

Expect fear to show up.
Not just fear of failure, but also fear of success.
Fear of outgrowing familiar circles.
Fear of being seen differently.
Fear of sustaining your own standards without an external structure to lean on or blame.

Entrepreneurship doesn't just expose weaknesses. It exposes power. Power that has always been in you, but contained for years.

The Three Phases of an Identity Shift

Recognition
Recognition is the moment misalignment becomes impossible to ignore. The internal awakening where growth demands honesty. This is where old operating patterns surface clearly:

> Approval-seeking
> Fear of judgment
> Perfectionism
> Outdated conditioning

Nothing changes until it's named.

Reclamation
Reclamation is the process of taking back what was set aside to fit into roles, expectations, or environments that no longer serve. This is where confidence is rebuilt and leadership instincts are reclaimed.

"Tell me what to do" becomes "What do I choose?"
"I need to get this right" becomes "I need to move."
"I can't mess this up" becomes "Everything is data."

Confidence isn't gifted.
It's trained.

Reinforcement
Reinforcement is where identity becomes embodied. New habits, boundaries, environments, and behaviors make the shift real. This is where consistency turns the new self into the default.

The posture becomes:

Direct
Clear
Self-honoring
Guarded
Decisive
Vision-forward

Explaining stops.
Building begins.
Leadership takes form.

Identity shifts don't happen in theory. They show up on the calendar.

If time is still allocated 100% to the job and 0% to the dream, life will continue reflecting exactly that.

The CEO shift requires redefining time.
Start small:

    5 hours a week
    3 mornings a week
    1 evening a week
    One focused weekend session

This isn't about volume. It's about consistency. A business grows in protected time, not discovered time.

SMART QUIT REALITY CHECK

Where am I still waiting for permission?

What am I afraid will change if I fully step into who I am?

Where does leadership already show up naturally and effortlessly?

What part of myself is ready to stop apologizing?

––––––––––––––––––

Identity work isn't about becoming someone new.
It's about returning to who you've always been.

Real People. Real Quits. Real Wins.

Michelle Zatlyn

Smart Quit Age: 30 years old (co-founded Cloudflare in 2009)
Education: B.S. in Chemistry; M.B.A.
Economic Background: Middle-class upbringing; parents were small business owners

After earning her MBA at Harvard Business School, Michelle Zatlyn worked at Google, surrounded by some of the smartest people in the technology field. But instead of settling into a comfortable corporate path, she started noticing a massive problem that no one seemed to be solving; how to make the internet more secure, faster, and more reliable for everyone.

With friends she met while at Harvard, Michelle began exploring an idea that would eventually become Cloudflare. What started as a class project quickly evolved into a startup concept. Michelle made the bold decision to leave the stability of Google to pursue her startup company full-time.

Michelle carefully planned her exit from Google. She spoke to mentors, mapped out what she needed financially and professionally, and made sure to leave with strong relationships intact. Her messaging to her peers and supervisors was respectful and visionary: she emphasized that she was leaving, not because of dissatisfaction, but to solve a big, meaningful problem.

In 2009, Michelle and her co-founders launched Cloudflare with the mission to help build a better internet. What began as a risky leap turned into one of Silicon Valley's most successful tech stories, a public company now protecting websites globally. Millions of websites use Cloudflare including major brands like Shopify, IBM and Zendesk, it has over $1 billion in annual revenue and is seen as a key competitor to Amazon Web Services in edge computing and security.

Michelle's departure from Google led to creating a company that successfully scaled globally and trusted with credibility in the developer and enterprise community.

Whether you think you can, or you think you can't, you're right.
Henry Ford

CHAPTER NINETEEN
IDENTITY → ACTION → INCOME

Many people expect the first 90 days of entrepreneurship to feel like freedom, ease, open space, inspiration, and clarity. In reality, the first 90 days feel like everything at once; the good, the hard, and the uncomfortable. Capability and uncertainty coexist. Excitement runs alongside exhaustion. Liberation comes with heightened awareness. Motivation collides with overwhelm.

This was not simply a career change. It was a shift in the center of gravity of life itself. Stabilizing energy, building rhythm, and creating forward motion without burnout or spiraling becomes the real work of this season.

There is one primary objective in the first 90 days. Not earning six figures. Not a perfect brand. Not scaling. Not launching endlessly. The goal is consistency and confidence around your offer or product. Confidence creates clarity. Clarity creates demand. Demand creates profit. A business becomes real through repetition, not constant reinvention.

Since the foundation of the first 90 days is the CEO schedule, it's important to recognize that structure, not pressure, creates stability.

A sustainable weekly rhythm is built around four pillars:
Client or Customer Work, Visibility, Sales, and CEO Time.

PILLAR	PURPOSE	EXAMPLE
Client or Customer Work	Deliver the transformation	2–3 time blocks/week
Visibility	Stay seen and searchable	3 posts/week or 3 outreach/day
Sales	Invitations & conversations	Daily intentional connection
CEO Time	Planning, reflection, direction	1–2 hours/week

When a schedule includes only:

Client work → growth stalls

Content → revenue starves

Sales → delivery suffocates

Planning → progress procrastinates

All four must exist together, consistently and sustainably.

Client and customer work pays the bills and, early on, can dominate the calendar. This work builds reputation, validates the business, and produces results. It belongs in CEO time because it reveals what works, what doesn't, and what clients and customers value most. However, even this must be intentionally capped. Too much delivery leaves no space for growth. The aim is honoring commitments while protecting margin to build the business behind the scenes.

Digital content functions as the visibility engine. It attracts the audience, builds trust, and establishes authority. In early-stage entrepreneurship, content is marketing and is treated as CEO work, not just filler between tasks. Content clarifies messaging, sharpens voice, and increases demand. Without consistent visibility, pipelines dry up. Content created today becomes sales tomorrow.

Visibility does not require performance, loudness, dancing online, or oversharing, unless that fits the brand. Visibility means showing up intentionally where the right people already are. A simple rule applies: post or reach out before scrolling. A thought. A lesson. A question. A behind-the-scenes moment. A simple "here's what's being built."

Visibility is presence, not performance.

Sales are service. Sales are products. Sales are the lifeblood of a business and deserve protected CEO time. In the early stages, every conversation, follow-up, and offer refinement builds understanding and generates bridge income. Sales reveal how the market responds and where adjustments are needed.

Sales are not convincing, begging, pitching, or hoping to be liked. Sales are letting the right people know help is available. A starting goal is simple: one meaningful conversation per day.

One check-in. One follow-up. One invitation. One response.

One per day equals thirty per month. Thirty per month builds a pipeline. A pipeline creates peace.

Planning is where control returns to the calendar. Planning shifts work from reaction to leadership. This time is used to set priorities, review numbers, assess what's working, and adjust before problems compound. Without planning, drift sets in. With planning, execution sharpens.

During this period, the urge to change the offer or constantly create product iterations will surface, especially when affirmation feels absent or results feel slow. The discipline is anchoring. Repetition builds recognition. Recognition builds demand. Demand builds referrals. Confusion erodes progress. Consistency compounds it. Your product or service is the story being told to the market, and that story must be told long enough to be understood.

The 90-Day Focus Formula

1 || One Audience

2 || One Offer

3 || One Platform (primary visibility + consistency)

4 || One Measurable Goal

The 90-day focus is narrow by design.

Everything else is noise.

Emotionally, these 90 days may sound like:

> "This isn't working."
> "Maybe this was a mistake."
> "Why is this taking so long?"
> "Oh wait, this is working."

This is stretching, not failure. Your nervous system is learning something new, safety without external validation. Decisions are being made without permission. Rest is being taken without guilt. Leadership is becoming internal.

Support systems matter deeply in this phase. Not echo chambers. Not cheer squads. Not constant advice. Steady voices. Grounded reminders. You should always have at least one person in your corner who can say, "This is normal," "Stay with it," "Preparation happened for a reason," "Don't quit now."

Smart Quitters are not meant to travel alone. Isolation is where doubt grows. Stability is built through rhythm, structure, and support, one consistent day at a time.

Your purpose is not fragile.
Your calling is not temporary.
Your success is not accidental.
Your potential is just getting started.

SMART QUIT REALITY CHECK

What time will I work on my business each week?

Where will I show up consistently?

What offer am I repeating for at least 90 days?

Who is in my support circle?

———————————————

These four decisions create your trajectory.

Real People. Real Quits. Real Wins.

Daymond John

Smart Quit Age: 23 (founded FUBU in 1992)
Education: High School Diploma
Economic Background: Working class. Single mother. Divorced parents.

Daymond John's entrepreneurial journey was not a glamorous leap, but a strategic, scrappy, disciplined transition fueled by vision and relentless execution. Though his entrepreneurial fire showed early, like many future founders, he didn't have the luxury of quitting his job to chase a dream. He had responsibilities, bills, and reality staring him straight in the face.

After high school, Daymond worked at Red Lobster, clocking long shifts while building ideas between tables. This wasn't a dead-end job for him; it was his runway. Every paycheck became startup capital. Every shift bought him more time to refine the business he believed he could build.

That business was FUBU, For Us, By Us, a clothing brand created for the hip-hop community at a time when mainstream fashion ignored or misrepresented Black culture. Daymond started with a simple MVP: handmade wool hats. No fashion background. No manufacturing experience. No investors. Just hustle, testing, iteration, and listening closely to what people wanted.

He tested product-market fit on the streets of Queens. Then he expanded to T-shirts, as he ran operations from his mother's house. His mother played a critical role, remortgaging her home to give him $100,000 in capital when banks wouldn't take him seriously.

Daymond didn't quit Red Lobster until FUBU had consistent demand. That's Smart Quit™ discipline. He built his business in layers: awareness through hip-hop artists, resonance through street culture, and authority through strategic placements in music videos and tours.

The turning point came when LL Cool J, also from Queens, wore FUBU in a Gap commercial without being paid by FUBU. It was a cultural disruption and brand breakthrough. Suddenly, the world took notice. FUBU scaled into global distribution, landing deals that pushed the brand into major retailers and international markets.

FUBU ultimately generated over $6 billion in sales.

Daymond didn't build FUBU by following the rules of the fashion industry; he rewrote them. He built demand through culture, not catalogs. Through authenticity, not access. Through community, not corporations.

Today, many know him as a star on Shark Tank, but his real influence is deeper. He represents a new entrepreneur, one rooted in resourcefulness, cultural intelligence, and the ability to turn scarcity into strategy.

CHAPTER TWENTY
BUILDING SUSTAINABLE DEMAND

Demand is not built by yelling online, launching ten offers at once, chasing every trend, or trying to be everywhere for everyone. Demand is built through consistency, clarity, resonance, rhythmic visibility, and responsibility to the message. People typically don't buy the first time they see something. They buy when trust is established and trust is built over time. Consistency is a currency that builds credibility.

Demand is not an algorithm problem. The solution is not going viral, perfect branding, or even daily posting. Demand is created when the right people consistently experience a brand as reliable, grounded, clear, useful, believable, and value-driven. Buying happens when the solution feels obvious. It becomes the obvious answer from repetition of message and mastery of a clear lane.

Demand Grows in Three Layers

Awareness
Awareness is the first layer of demand: simple recognition. At this stage, presence matters more than polish. The goal is visibility, placing the message, work, and offer in front of the people who need it. Demand cannot grow if no one knows the brand exists. Awareness puts the name of a brand

on the map. Performing, impressing, or simply being seen in the room is not the priority. It's important to prioritize consistent presence so your name, face, and offer become familiar. Everything is shared plainly and repeatedly.

Resonance

Resonance is the second layer, where visibility turns into connection. This is the point where people don't just see the message, they feel it. The language lands. Your story mirrors your future customer's experience. Resonance happens when someone thinks, "That's me," or "This person gets it." It is the emotional bridge between what's being offered and what's needed. Resonance turns followers into believers and believers into buyers. Without resonance, visibility is noise. With it, presence becomes magnetic. This layer is built through language, tone, lived experience, and point of view. It is identity connection.

Authority

Authority is the third and most powerful layer of demand. Trust is established. Credibility is proven. The brand becomes a reference point. Authority comes from mastery, repetition, results, case studies, testimonials, confidence, and clarity of perspective. It's not about perfection; it's about reliability. When authority is present, chasing clients stops and inbound demand begins. Authority is what makes demand sustainable, scalable, and long-term. Authority isn't loud. Authority is felt.

Demand doesn't grow by accident as awareness moves into resonance and then authority. It grows through consistency, showing up in a way audiences can depend on. The road from awareness to authority is paved with visibility that is rhythmic, repeatable, and sustainable. I did not say heavy, forced, or sporadic. When visibility becomes a steady drumbeat instead of an occasional push, presence compounds, messages spread, and authority takes root.

DAY/TIME	FOCUS	EXAMPLE
1-2 x per week	Teach	A lesson, insight, how-to, explanation
1-2 x per week	Show	Behind the scenes, real process, client work
1-2 x per week	Call In	If this is where you are, here's your next step

Does this sound like entertainment? No, this is education and normalization of a voice in your audience's world.

The key is repetition of a clear message. Make your offer memorable by repeating a consistent, clear offer that answers:

1 || Who you serve

2 || What you help them do

3 || Why your way works

4 || What are the results

Your message must be delivered the same or similar way for at least 90 days. Audiences need repetition. Brands need consistency. Identity needs reinforcement. Constantly changing a message to avoid discomfort trades impact for insecurity. You should make a commitment that any trade-offs end here.

People also buy from businesses that make them feel seen, safe, and supported. This is emotional safety.

Every audience is silently asking:
Can this company and product or service be trusted?
Is there real understanding here?
Is this a long-term solution?

Those questions are answered through presence, not perfection and that expectation lives internally, not externally. No one is paying for flawlessness. What customers want is understanding, guidance, support, and meaningful delivery. Humanity builds trust. Imperfection creates relatability. Growth creates aspiration. That balance is the brand.

The question to hold is simple: What should your name represent?
When people hear your brand, the association should be clarity, confidence, stability, transformation, ease, and power. Whatever experience your business is designed to deliver.

Reputation grows demand.

SMART QUIT REALITY CHECK

When people experience me or my product, what do I want them to feel?

What message do I want to be known for repeating?

What is the simplest visibility rhythm I can commit to weekly?

What platform or space feels most natural for me to show up consistently?

This is your demand engine.
Not hustle.
Not noise.
Presence with precision.

Real People. Real Quits. Real Wins.

Apoorva Mehta

Smart Quit Age: 26 years old (launched Instacart in 2012)
Education: B.S. in Electrical Engineering
Economic Background: Middle-class upbringing. No generational wealth, no entrepreneurial background.

Apoorva Mehta's story is the definition of disciplined experimentation, strategic resilience, and the Smart Quit™ philosophy lived out in real time. Born in India and raised in Canada, Apoorva grew up in a household that valued education, stability, and technical skill. He followed the expected path, studying electrical engineering. He was smart, analytical, and driven, and he entered the workforce with the same precision that defined his thinking. But his early career wasn't glamorous.

Apoorva worked as an engineer at BlackBerry, Qualcomm, and eventually Amazon. At Amazon, he worked on the fulfillment systems that powered the company's logistics network, the foundation of his understanding of e-commerce, supply chain, and complex systems design. That job became his training ground, teaching him how to think at scale, build infrastructure, and recognize inefficiencies others overlooked.

Still, Apoorva knew he wasn't meant to stay in a traditional job. He felt the familiar tension many Smart Quit™ entrepreneurs feel: "I'm good at this, but it's not my calling." Instead of quitting impulsively or romanticizing entrepreneurship, he made a plan.

In 2010, he quit his job at Amazon and moved to San Francisco to become a founder, not because he had the perfect idea, but because he had the appetite to test relentlessly.

What followed was a gauntlet of experimentation. Apoorva built 20 failed startups in two years. Yes, twenty. The failures ranged from social networks for lawyers to analytics tools to advertising platforms. Most people would have quit after three. Or five. Or ten. But Apoorva wasn't chasing validation; he was chasing clarity. Each failure sharpened his instincts. Each misstep taught him what problems were too small, too crowded, or too boring to sustain real momentum.

His Smart Quit™ moment didn't come from quitting his job, it came from quitting bad ideas fast enough to find the right one. His breakthrough arrived in 2012, when Apoorva realized something simple but powerful: even in the heart of Silicon Valley, grocery shopping was a hassle. People valued convenience in everything except groceries. There was no seamless way to have them delivered on demand. And while large companies had flirted with the concept, no one had cracked the code.

Apoorva saw an opening, a massive market, a daily need, and a logistics problem he was uniquely equipped to solve. Drawing from his Amazon experience, he built an MVP for Instacart in just a few weeks. He coded the early version of the app himself. He tested the product by delivering groceries to himself. He focused on one core promise: groceries delivered in under two hours.

He didn't start with warehouses, fleets, or heavy infrastructure. He started with lean systems, a simple app, and local stores. This was Smart Quit™ in action: build small, test fast, and validate demand before expanding.

He applied to Y Combinator, the top startup accelerator in the U.S., famously late. The application deadline had passed. So he sent them a link: an Instacart order. Within 30 minutes, a bag of groceries arrived at the Y Combinator office. It was the most practical, undeniable demonstration of product-market fit. They accepted him.

Once in YC, Instacart exploded. People didn't just want the product, they needed it. The early model was brilliant: crowd-sourced shoppers, no warehouses, strategic partnerships with grocers, and software that optimized routes, batching, and delivery windows. Apoorva built a logistics engine disguised as a grocery app.

Its growth was steady, then explosive, especially when the pandemic hit in 2020 and Instacart became an essential service. Demand surged by over 400%. Under Apoorva's leadership, the company scaled into a multi-billion-dollar platform, serving millions of households and partnering with thousands of retailers.

What makes his story uniquely Smart Quit™ is this: Apoorva didn't quit his career to "follow his passion." He quit once he built mastery. He quit once he had evidence. He quit once he understood the problem only he could solve. His path shows that quitting isn't the first step. It's the strategic step. He used corporate life as a training ground, failure as data, and experimentation as his proving system. Instacart wasn't a stroke of luck; it was the result of relentless revision, operational insight, and the patience to wait for the right idea, not just any idea.

In 2021, after leading Instacart's rise to becoming one of the most valuable private companies in America, Apoorva stepped down as CEO, another Smart Quit™ moment. He shifted from operator to executive chairman, allowing leadership more aligned with Instacart's next chapter to step in. He understood something many founders don't. Founding requires one skillset; scaling requires another.

Stage Four:
PROFIT

188

You do not rise to the level of your goals.
You fall to the level of your systems.
James Clear, Atomic Habits

CHAPTER TWENTY-ONE
BREATHE WHILE YOU GROW

Scaling does not mean longer hours, more offers, constant posting, or grinding harder. Scaling is doing less with a greater impact. It means setting standards that protect your sanity, building systems that carry the work, and making decisions like a leader, no longer as a laborer.

If growth requires exhaustion, it isn't growth. It's self-abandonment. Chaos does not scale. You must get organized first, then elevate. The real capacity question isn't, "How much can be handled?" It's, "What no longer needs to be done personally?" That shift is where delegation, systemization, boundaries, and leadership begin.

A business cannot expand while one person functions as the assistant, strategist, executor, administrator, and support desk. At some point, leadership must replace overfunctioning.

The Three Systems Required to Scale

Delivery System

A delivery system is how an offer is fulfilled. A strong delivery system is consistent, predictable, and repeatable. Reinventing the process for every client or customer creates labor, not a business.

A scalable delivery system clearly defines:

> **Client Experience & Outcomes:** How clients/customers experience the work and what results they receive.

> **Process & Operations:** The step-by-step workflow that ensures consistency and efficiency.

> **Capacity & Scalability:** How much can be delivered without bottlenecks and how the system grows with demand.

> **Rhythm & Structure:** The predictable cadence and flow that keeps delivery smooth.

> **Measurement & Feedback:** How success is tracked, evaluated, and optimized over time.

> **Experience Ownership:** Who is accountable for each part of the client journey and overall satisfaction.

How does this delivery system protect your time, energy, and resources while maximizing results? This becomes your signature process.

Sales System
This is how new customers find the business and convert. It is not cold pitching, begging, DM blasting, or performance-driven selling. It is a consistent visibility rhythm, a clear invitation, a follow-up habit, and a trustworthy presence.

A scalable sales system clearly defines:

> **Lead Generation & Attraction:** How prospects discover the business and become aware of the offer.
> **Conversion & Follow-Up:** The steps that move prospects from interest to commitment.

Offer Clarity & Messaging: How the value is communicated consistently and persuasively.

Cadence & Predictability: The regular rhythm of outreach, follow-ups, and opportunities.

Measurement & Optimization: How results are tracked, analyzed, and improved over time.

Ownership & Accountability: Who manages each stage of the sales process and ensures outcomes.

A healthy sales system feels light and repeatable, not forced or complex.

Support System
This system protects time and energy. It includes calendar boundaries, communication norms, onboarding and offboarding, automation, templates, and clearly defined expectations.

A scalable support system clearly defines:

Time & Energy Protection: Boundaries, communication norms, and delegation to prevent overload.

Processes & Automations: Templates, systems, and workflows that handle repetitive tasks efficiently.

Onboarding & Offboarding: How clients, customers, and team members are introduced and transitioned.

Issue Resolution & Escalation: Clear protocols for addressing challenges or exceptions.

Measurement & Feedback: How support success is tracked and improved.

Ownership & Responsibility: Who ensures operations run smoothly and client/customer needs are met.

Strong support systems remove emotional labor, decision fatigue, confusion, and overfunctioning preventing burnout before it starts.

Systems don't restrict freedom.
Systems create it.

A mature business feels rhythmic, predictable, and stable. That is what sustainability looks like.

CEO Boundary Standards for Scale

BEGINNER BUSINESS	SCALED BUSINESS
"I do everything manually."	"I work from templates & structure."
"Every client is different."	"I provide personalized outcomes through repeatable processes."
"I take every opportunity."	"I choose what aligns with vision and capacity."
"I respond when things happen."	"I operate from proactive rhythm."

As you scale, some of the CEO boundary standards that must be adopted are:
No rushing to respond
No explaining or justifying boundaries
No negotiating value
No carrying emotional weight that doesn't belong to the role
No self-abandonment to meet expectations

This isn't attitude.
It's self-respect in operation.

Leadership begins with self-leadership. When the time comes to hire, the instinct is often to bring on marketing, sales, or branding support. But the first hire (part-time or contract) should be the role that creates the most capacity for you to lead. Early support should amplify the owner role, not distract from it.

In most cases, that first hire is an Operations or Administrative Support role. This role protects the calendar, manages communication, maintains structure, and keeps momentum steady. When systems replace dependence on a single person, scalability becomes possible.
As growth continues, self-preservation remains non-negotiable. This is the rule: if it costs you peace, joy, rest, relationships, or health, the cost is too much. Scaling is not about expanding the business at all costs. It's about expanding capacity through boundaries, systems, support, standards, and internal leadership.

A business will only grow to the level of leadership the owner is willing to embody.

Your next level is not in doing more. Your next level is in leading more.
You are not building a job. You are building a company.
You are building a legacy.

SMART QUIT REALITY CHECK

Where am I still doing work someone else could handle?

What process in my business needs to be standardized next?

What boundaries would immediately create more energy if I honored them?

Who can I bring in (contract, part-time, task-based) to support my expansion?

Real People. Real Quits. Real Wins.

Serena Williams

Smart Quit Age: 35 years old (launched Serena Ventures in 2014, while still competing in tennis professionally)
Education: High school graduate and business certifications
Economic Background: Parents coached her tennis career from a very young age

Serena Williams didn't just dominate tennis, she redefined what power, persistence, and purpose could look like. At the peak of her athletic career, she started asking herself a bigger question: What comes next?

Between Grand Slam titles and global tours, she began sitting in on meetings with brand partners, learning the mechanics of business deals, and paying attention to how companies grew. She noticed how few founders looked like her or had access to the same rooms. That realization became her turning point.

In 2014, while still competing, Serena founded Serena Ventures, a venture capital firm built to invest in women, people of color, and underrepresented founders. She used her platform not just for profit, but for purpose to bridge the gap between opportunity and access.

At first, many underestimated her assuming she was just "dabbling" in investing. But Serena approached business the same way she approached tennis: with relentless preparation and unshakable confidence. She studied founders, built a team of seasoned investors, and began strategically backing companies she believed in.

Today, Serena Ventures has invested in more than 85 companies, including Impossible Foods, MasterClass, Noom, and Daily Harvest. Her portfolio represents billions in enterprise value and has opened doors for founders historically left out of venture capital.
But Serena didn't stop there. She launched her own fashion line, S by Serena,

celebrating strength and style for all body types; became a part-owner of Angel City FC, a women's soccer team; and continues to champion equity in sports, business, and beyond.

Her journey isn't just about leaving one career for another it's about expanding what's possible. Serena Williams didn't retire. She reinvented. She didn't quit. She built her next chapter smarter, stronger, and entirely on her own terms.

CHAPTER TWENTY-TWO
BUILDING A MOMENT V. BUILDING A LIFETIME

Smart Quitter's goal isn't to leave one job only to recreate the same struggle under a different title. The work done up to this point is not meant for survival mode, waking up anxious each month, scraping by, or building a business that owns its founder. The purpose is to create wealth, freedom, peace, and legacy.

Legacy isn't defined by money alone. Legacy is what continues to function and provide value without constant presence. This requires learning how to:

> Price with integrity
> Protect time alongside profit
> Build assets instead of only selling effort
> Ensure the business outlives the energy that fuels it
> Shift from earning to survive to building to sustain.

Income is not wealth. Some earn over $100K and remain broke; others earn $50K and are positioned for long-term wealth. Money alone does not create wealth. What is done with money does.

Income = Money earned

Profit = Money kept

Wealth = Money that grows independently of your labor

Scaling and wealth creation cannot occur under undervaluation. Undercharging, overdelivering, overfunctioning, discounting, or pricing for approval instead of sustainability leads to burnout, resentment, and instability. Pricing is not a reflection of personal worth. It is an exercise in responsibility. It should support well-being, growth, and sustainable business operations.

Pricing should reflect:

Clarity provided
Energy invested
Transformation delivered
The life being built

Pricing should not be determined by:

Market comparison exclusively
Fear of rejection
Perceived affordability
Impostor syndrome
Approval of others

Products and services are not transactions. They provide access to clarity, relief, confidence, identity shifts, regained time, or a better way of living. That is the value.

Wealth will require you to honor boundaries:

Time Boundaries: Time is not freely available; the calendar reflects intentional prioritization.

Energy Boundaries: If something costs peace, it costs too much.

Client/Customer Boundaries: Guidance is offered, but ownership of action belongs to the client or customer.

Financial Boundaries: Every dollar has a purpose. Spending is stewardship, not a soothing mechanism.

The transition from earned income to asset income is essential. Early revenue relies on labor, energy, expertise, and presence... earned income. Over time, the focus shifts to assets: digital products, frameworks, courses, communities, brand partnerships, speaking engagements, equity, and automated sales channels. Assets create income without constant input, enabling sustainable scaling.

Scaling is not about working harder; it is about building systems and assets that perform independently. Discipline underpins this work. Discipline is not punishment. It is a devotion to your future self.

Discipline looks like:

Respecting your schedule (you and others)
Showing up consistently, even without external oversight
Taking small, repeated actions
Making long-term decisions over emotional reactions

Legacies are built not through intensity, but through repeatable, grounded, consistent action.

SMART QUIT REALITY CHECK

What is being built that will last beyond my direct effort?

Which parts of my business can be transformed into assets instead of effort?

Which boundaries, if honored, would immediately increase profit?

What identity aligns with my long-term vision and legacy?

———————————

Your mission extends beyond business: it will build a life of honor, create wealth that sustains, and establish a legacy that reflects the person you will be.

This is the work. This is the path. This is the long game.

Real People. Real Quits. Real Wins.

Barbara Corcoran

Smart Quit Age: 24 years old (founded The Corcoran Group in 1973)
Education: B.A. in Education
Economic Background: Grew up in a working-class, lower-income (One of 10 children, Dad worked various jobs, mom was a stay at home mom)

Barbara Corcoran's success didn't start with privilege or a business plan, it started with a tray of coffee cups and a dream she didn't yet know she had. At 23, she was working as a waitress at a diner in New Jersey when a man she'd been serving offered her something unexpected: a $1,000 loan and the idea that she should try real estate.

It was a bold proposition, especially for a young woman who had never taken a business course, had no experience in sales, and was barely making rent. But Barbara's instincts told her to say yes. He became her boyfriend and she quit her job, moved to New York City, and launched a tiny real estate venture with him from their one-bedroom apartment.

It was called The Corcoran-Simonè Company and for seven years Barbara hustled to make it work. She cold-called clients, studied the market, and used creativity to outsmart her competition. While other agents focused on luxury listings, Barbara leaned into personality and positioning, creating a reputation for being bold, sharp, and refreshingly different in a male-dominated industry.

Then came the breakup that would change everything. Her boyfriend and business partner announced he was leaving her and starting his own firm with their receptionist. The personal betrayal stung, but it was his parting words that lit the fire: "You'll never succeed without me."

Barbara decided to prove him wrong. She took her half of the business, walked away from both the relationship and the company they'd built together, and rebranded herself overnight. The Corcoran Group was born. With nothing but her name, a desk, and the sheer will to win, Barbara began her new journey.

She leaned into marketing genius before marketing was even a buzzword. Barbara began publishing The Corcoran Report, one of the first real estate trend analyses in the U.S., which positioned her as an expert and made headlines across New York. She turned her setbacks into strategy, her story into leverage, and her confidence into currency.

By the mid-1980s, The Corcoran Group had become one of New York's premier real estate firms, known for its daring ads, media savvy, and customer-first reputation. Barbara was no longer just selling apartments, she was selling possibility. Her once small startup was suddenly handling multi-million-dollar listings for the city's elite.

In 2001, after nearly three decades of building, Barbara sold The Corcoran Group to NRT (now Realogy) for $66 million, transforming herself from a girl who waited tables, to one of the most successful self-made women in business.

But she didn't stop there. Barbara reinvented herself again as an investor, author, motivational speaker, and TV personality. When she joined Shark Tank, she became the heart and soul of the show known for her quick wit, tough love, and compassion for scrappy founders who remind her of where she started.

Today, Barbara Corcoran stands as a living example of what it means to quit smart. She didn't just walk away from a job, she walked away from a version of herself that no longer fit. From waitress to mogul, from heartbreak to headline, her story is a masterclass in turning rejection into reinvention.

CHAPTER TWENTY-THREE
JUST MOVE.

The door has been unlocked. Now you choose.

You didn't read this book because you were bored.

You read it because something in you was already shifting.

A knowing.

A pull.

A quiet truth that refused to stay quiet.

You didn't come here to dream about another life.

You came because the life you've been living is too small for who you're becoming.

You are not leaving your job.

You are leaving the version of you who needed permission to live.

Every chapter of your story, every role, every skill, every hard lesson has prepared you for your next level.

You are not behind.

You were being built.

Built to:

Think with clarity

Lead with courage

Choose with intention

Build with discipline

Stand in your purpose

Your calling is not fragile.

Your dream is not accidental.

Your future is not a gamble.

You know what alignment feels like now.

You know what settling costs.

You know what staying small does to your spirit.

Fear is natural.

Doubt is human.

But neither of them are allowed to drive.

You do.

You don't need to rush.

You don't need to prove anything.

You don't need to explain your decision to anyone who cannot see your potential.

You just need to move.

Move with strategy.

Move with clarity.

Move with peace.

Move with the confidence of a winner who knows their purpose will be enough.

This is the end of this book.

But the beginning of your next chapter.

So go.

Move.

Smart Quit.

EPILOGUE

Your new life will cost you your old one.
Brianna Wiest

THE SECRET SAUCE
My Why

Disclaimer: Your results may vary if your recipe for success doesn't include the ingredient I consider my "secret sauce". The One I credit for everything I've built.

But remember the Lord your God,
for it is He who gives you the ability to produce wealth...
Deuteronomy 8:18 (NIV)

My faith is woven into everything I do, but I've placed this story here, in the Epilogue, so the value of Smart Quit remains accessible to anyone on their own path - whether they share my beliefs or not.

The name of the company that owns my business coaching franchise and publishing company, Eight18 is derived from Deuteronomy 8:18, which states:

But remember the LORD your God is the one who makes you wealthy. He's confirming the promise which he swore to your ancestors. It's still in effect to-day.

My entire entrepreneurial journey has been a faith walk, something I believe God called me into, and something I have chosen to walk in obedience - including Smart Quit. I believe it would be a mistake to omit the role faith has played, because as the saying goes, "favor ain't fair." Much of the success I've experienced has been divinely orchestrated. But it always begins with obedience.

I want to close this book by sharing one of the faith moments that shaped everything that has unfolded for me since.

When I first stepped out on faith, leaving my six-figure job to invest in a business coaching franchise, my plan was to transition gradually, supported by the closing of a real estate deal that was supposed to provide a financial cushion. But life had other plans. When I told my boss that I was starting my own business, she informed me that Friday would be my last day. And the real estate deal? It never closed.

Within a year, I went from a six-figure salary to six figures in debt.

Fast forward 11 months, I finally secured my first client and received my first payment of $12,000. The next morning, I sat at my desk debating whether to tithe. A tithe is simply the practice of giving 10% of your income back to your church as an act of worship, gratitude, and support for the ministry.

And let me tell you, I needed every cent of that money. As a single woman with one income, a mortgage, car payment, living expenses, and growing business costs, the weight was real.

But in that moment, God reminded me of my tithing journey in my 20s and made it clear: Don't start failing tests you have already learned to pass.
So, without hesitation, I opened my church's giving app and tithed $1,200.
Three hours later, I received my first lead from my franchiser, my second client.
Three days later, I received a second lead, from a major corporation in Dallas requesting a Certified Implementer with over three years of experience. At that time, I had less than one year experience and no certification. By every natural standard, I should not have qualified. But God doesn't require qualifications. He requires obedience.

The Vice President met with me for six hours. His team became my third client. And that VP, now corprepreneur, is a friend, partner and mentor.

Three weeks later, I received my first referral from a colleague, who became not only one of my favorite clients, but hired me for two of their companies. Clients #4 and #8.

I am not saying God is a vending machine; insert tithe, receive miracle, but I do believe that what I consider a miracle grew from the $1,200 seed of obedience I planted that day.

To put it in perspective:
Those first four clients accounted for $165,000 in revenue that year alone.

God is still in the miracle-working business.

So if you are reading this and you feel like you are on the brink of giving up, If you feel alone, if you feel like you can't make it, let this be your reminder:
You can.
You are not alone.

The test you are facing right now can become your testimony.

I hope reading Smart Quit has been as transformative for you, as writing it has been for me.

Drea Lynn

**Today is the first day of the rest of your life.
Make it count.**

**Started From the Bottom
Now They're Here**
(Entrepreneurs Just Like You)

Mikaila Ulmer, Me & the Bees Lemonade
Founding Age: age 4
Education: Kindergarten
Economic Background: Parents have business degrees and provided Mikaila support as she developed her business.
Work History: Owned a lemonade stand

Fred DeLuca, Subway
Founding Age: age 17
Education: High School
Economic Background: Financially challenged, he collected empty soda bottles to earn money and his entrepreneurial spirit led him to seek ways to fund college.
Work History: Worked at a hardware store.

Mark Zuckerberg, Facebook
Founding Age: age 19
Education: College Dropout (sophomore at Harvard when he launched Facebook)
Economic Background: Comfortable financial environment
Work History: Largely technical and programming-focused (student work)

Whitney Wolfe Herd, Tinder, Bumble
Founding Age: age 22, age 25 (Bumble)
Education: Bachelor's Degree (Southern Methodist University)
Economic Background: Family was wealthy, father is a property developer
Work History: Executive (Vice President of Marketing)

Katrina Lake, Stich Fix
Smart Quit Age: age 28
Education: B.A. in Economics (Stanford) MBA (Harvard)
Economic Background: Middle-class family, father was a physician and her mother was an artist.
Work History: Consultant, Research Analyst, Retail, Business Strategy

Rhianna, Fenty Beauty
Smart Quit Age: age 29
Education: High School dropout (left to focus on her music career)
Economic Background: Working-class family. Family faced financial challenges and father struggled with addiction.
Work History: Successful and groundbreaking musical artist

Jessica Alba, The Honest Company
Smart Quit Age: age 29 years old
Education: High school graduate, Studied acting at the Atlantic Theater Company
Economic Background: Grew up in a working-class family;
Her mother was a lifeguard and homemaker; her father served in the U.S. Air Force and later worked in real estate.
Work History: Actress (early career started at age 13)

Oprah, Harpo Productions
Smart Quit Age: age 32
Education: Bachelor's Degree
Economic Background: Poverty, raised in extremely difficult circumstances including periods without indoor plumbing and she faced abuse and instability throughout her childhood
Work background: Media, reading the news on local radio, local news anchor, local daytime talk show host.

Martha Stewart, Martha Stewart Living
Smart Quit Age: age 35
Education: Bachelor's Degree
Economic Background: Working class, parents were educators. Stewart was involved in domestic activities like cooking and gardening.
Work History: Modeling, Stockbroker, Catering

Reid Hoffman, LinkedIn
Smart Quit Age: age 35
Education: Bachelor's Degree, Master's Degree
Economic Background: Middle class, parents were both lawyers and political activists.
Work History: Apple, Fujitsu, SocialNet.com, PayPal (COO)

Reed Hastings, Netflix
Smart Quit Age: age 37
Education: Bachelor's Degree, Master's Degree
Economic Background: Middle Class, father was in the military and mother was a mathematician.
Work Background: Peace Corps, teacher

Vera Wang, Vera Wang Fashion Design
Smart Quit Age: age 40
Education: Bachelor's Degree
Economic Background: Wealthy Chinese-American family. Father was a success entrepreneur in the pharmaceutical and petroleum industries and her mother worked as a translator for the United Nations.
Work Background: Fashion editor (Vogue), Accessories designer (Ralph Lauren)

CASE STUDIES & SOURCES

Steve Wozniak (pg. 16)
Encyclopedia Britannica. "Steve Wozniak."
Encyclopedia Britannica. "Apple Inc."
National Inventors Hall of Fame. "Steve Wozniak."
UC Berkeley College of Engineering. "Steve Wozniak: Inventor and Apple co-founder."
Biography.com. "Steve Wozniak."

Michelle Obama (pg. 31)
Encyclopedia Britannica. "Michelle Obama."
"Michelle Obama: Age, Education & Barack Obama." History.com
"Michelle Obama: Biography, First Lady, Philanthropist." Biography.com
"Michelle Obama." Wikipedia.
Obama, Michelle. Becoming. New York: Crown, 2018.

Mark Cuban (pg. 37)
"Mark Cuban." Wikipedia
"Mark Cuban." Biography.com
CNBC. "Mark Cuban had $82,000 stolen from his first company." CNBC Make It (Feb. 6, 2020)
CNBC. "Billionaire Mark Cuban on his success with Broadcast.com." CNBC (Apr. 4, 2021)
CNN Money. "Yahoo to buy Broadcast.com for $5.7B." CNN (Apr. 1, 1999)

Lisa Price (pg. 43)
"Carol's Daughter." Wikipedia.
Price, Lisa interview. "Carol's Daughter was born in the kitchen." ESSENCE (video interview/article).
Mackenzie, M. "Carol's Daughter Founder On Getting Comfortable With Fear..." Forbes (Nov. 1, 2017).
"L'Oréal USA Signs Agreement to Acquire Carol's Daughter." L'Oréal press release PDF (Oct. 20, 2014).
"Meet Our Founder, Lisa Price." Carol's Daughter
"How Lisa Price Turned Her Hobby Into a Natural Hair Care Empire." Northwestern Mutual.

"Carol's Daughter Founder Lisa Price Reflects…" Allure (interview).
"Fox Front to Black: Lisa Price, Founder of Carol's Daughter." Fox Business.

Marie Foreleo (pg. 50)
Marie Forleo. "About Marie Forleo." MarieForleo.com
Marie Forleo. "What's MarieTV?" MarieForleo.com
Marie Forleo. "B-School." MarieForleo.com

Sara Blakely (pg. 59)
O'Connor, Clare. "Undercover Billionaire: Sara Blakely Joins The Rich List Thanks To Spanx." Forbes (Mar. 7, 2012).
"Top Five Startup Tips From Spanx Billionaire Sara Blakely." Forbes (Apr. 2, 2012).
"How Sara Blakely of Spanx Turned $5,000 into $1 billion." Forbes (Mar. 26, 2012).
"Sara Blakely." Wikipedia (Spanish entry includes parents' occupations + communications degree).
"Sara Blakely on Resilience." Entrepreneur (interview/excerpts).
"The woman in control of America's bottom." The Guardian (Apr. 13, 2008).
Smith, Dave. "Billionaire Sara Blakely says she launched Spanx with just $5,000 from selling fax machines…" Fortune (Sept. 20, 2025).

Sophia Amoruso (pg. 69)
"Sophia Amoruso." Wikipedia.
Amoruso, Sophia. "My Story." SophiaAmoruso.com
Kay, Hellin. "Nasty Gal Founder Sophia Amoruso on How to Become a #GirlBoss." ELLE
"Nasty Gal CEO Sophia Amoruso: 'Wisdom is Earned Through Experience, Particularly Mistakes.'" Entrepreneur
Riddell, Roger. "Tech Cinderella story Nasty Gal is country's 'fastest growing retailer.'" Retail Dive
"Nasty Gal Founder Sophia Amoruso Talks About Company's Bankruptcy." Observer

Melanie Perkins (pg. 77)
"Canva." Wikipedia
"Melanie Perkins." Wikipedia.

BBC. "The 30-year-old woman who designed a $1bn business." BBC News (Jan. 10, 2018).
Startup News. "Yes We Canva - An Interview With Australia's Only Current Unicorn." StartupNews.com.au (2018).
The CEO Magazine. "How Canva became one of the most successful start-up unicorns in history." The CEO Magazine (Apr. 29, 2020).
The West Australian. "West Aussies take on tech world." The West Australian (profile/interview).

Anthony Wood (pg. 85)
"Anthony Wood (businessman)." Wikipedia
"Roku." Wikipedia

Eric Yuan (pg. 92)
Konrad, Alex. "Zoom, Zoom, Zoom! The Exclusive Inside Story..." Forbes (Apr. 19, 2019)
Rogers, Bruce. "Eric Yuan... left his job at Cisco to found Zoom in June of 2011." Forbes (Apr. 24, 2017).
High, Peter. "Zoom CEO's Promise To His Wife..." Forbes (Mar. 6, 2017)

Kevin Systrom (pg. 103)
Facebook (Meta). "Facebook to Acquire Instagram." About.fb.com (Apr. 9, 2012) Constine, Josh. "Instagram hits 1 billion monthly users..." TechCrunch (June 20, 2018)
"Facebook acquires Instagram for $1 billion..." CNN Business (Apr. 9, 2012)

Robert F. Smith (pg. 115)
Vista Equity Partners. "Robert F. Smith." VistaEquityPartners.com
Encyclopedia Britannica (Britannica Money). "Robert F. Smith."
Forbes. "Robert F. Smith." Forbes Profile
Cornell Chronicle. "Smith '85 to receive engineering college alumni honor."
CNBC. "Robert Smith, Delivering Alpha Speaker."
TIME. "Who Is Robert F. Smith?"

Leila Janah (pg. 126)
The Leila Janah Foundation. "Remembering Leila."
Sama. "Leila Janah's Story / Our Founder."
Wikipedia. "Leila Janah."
Heinz Awards. "Leila Janah."
"Leila Janah - Biography."
The Leila Janah Foundation. "Mission & Team / Our History."

Arlan Hamilton (pg. 137)
Backstage Capital. "For Investors" / "About"
Mascarenhas, Natasha. "200 investments in, Backstage Capital is pivoting to fund only existing portfolio companies." TechCrunch (May 5, 2022)
Delaney, Kevin. "Arlan Hamilton Went From Homeless to Running $20 Million in VC Funds. Here's How She Did It." TIME (Mar. 6, 2022)
"Arlan Hamilton." Wikipedia
"Arlan Hamilton founded VC firm Backstage Capital while homeless." CNBC (Nov. 19, 2018)

Justin Welsh (pg. 142)
Welsh, Justin. "About Me." JustinWelsh.me / Learn.JustinWelsh.me.
Welsh, Justin. "My complete $10M journey." JustinWelsh.me (June 7, 2025)
Welsh, Justin. "Subscribe to The Saturday Solopreneur." Learn.JustinWelsh.me.
"Justin Welsh." Startups.com Experts (bio: "coach SMB SaaS teams to $50M," sales leadership background).
"Justin Welsh Built a $7M Content Business With This Strategy." The Tilt

Tristan Walker (pg. 148)
Ha, Anthony. "Procter & Gamble acquires Walker & Company, Tristan Walker will remain as CEO." TechCrunch (Dec. 12, 2018).
"P&G (PG) Buys Walker & Company, Enhances Beauty Portfolio." NASDAQ (Dec. 13, 2018).
Cool, Kevin. "Tristan Walker." Stanford Graduate School of Business (Alumni Voices) (July 15, 2022).
"Tristan Walker (entrepreneur)." Wikipedia.
"Race in America: Entrepreneurship with Cheetie Kumar & Tristan Walker." The Washington Post Live (Dec. 2, 2021).

Andy Dunn (pg. 159)
"Andy Dunn." Wikipedia.
"Bonobos (apparel)." Wikipedia
De la Merced, Michael J. "Walmart to Buy Bonobos, Men's Wear Company, for $310 Million." The New York Times (June 16, 2017).
Reuters. "Walmart to Buy Bonobos for $310 Million." Fortune (June 16, 2017).
Case, Brendan (CNBC). "Walmart sells Bonobos to WHP Global and Express." CNBC (Apr. 13, 2023)

Michelle Zatlyn (pg. 169)
Forbes. "Michelle Zatlyn." Forbes Profile (updated June 3, 2025)
NASDAQ (Atlassian press release). "Atlassian Appoints Michelle Zatlyn… to Board of Directors"
Harvard Business School Alumni. Participant directory entry for Michelle Zatlyn
"Michelle Zatlyn." Wikipedia

Daymond John (pg. 177)
"Daymond John." Wikipedia
FUBU. "About – FUBU." FUBU.com
CNNMoney. "Daymond John on hip-hop, his mom and making it big." CNNMoney
Hilburn, Jair. "Daymond John Is On A Mission." Forbes (Jan. 17, 2022)

Apoorva Mehta (pg. 184)
Forbes. "Apoorva Mehta." Forbes Profile
Wikipedia. "Instacart."
Wang, Jennifer. "Instacart Founder Apoorva Mehta Becomes A Billionaire After New Funding Round." Forbes (June 17, 2020)
"Instacart founder launched 20 failed companies-now he's a billionaire." CNBC (Sept. 20, 2023)
The Indian Express. "Two Indians in US' Richest Entrepreneurs Under 40 list: Forbes." The Indian Express (Dec. 7, 2016)

Serena Williams (pg. 195)
Schulte-Bockum, Marie. "Serena Williams Joins Sorare…" Forbes
Williams, Serena. "Serena Ventures." SerenaVentures.com
"Serena Williams." Wikipedia
Ogus, Simon. "Serena Williams Announces Her VC Firm…" Forbes (Apr. 19, 2019)
Ha, Anthony. "Serena Williams' next act in venture capital…" TechCrunch (Aug. 15, 2022)

Barbara Corcoran (pg. 201)
Encyclopedia Britannica. "Barbara Corcoran."
"Barbara Corcoran." Wikipedia
Corcoran, Barbara. "About." BarbaraCorcoran.com
"Why Barbara Corcoran felt like a fraud after selling her business." CNBC Make It (Feb. 27, 2020)
"Barbara Corcoran - From waitress to real estate queen." Fortune (May 23, 2013)
"Barbara Corcoran: Real Winners Say 'Hit Me Again.'" Entrepreneur (Oct. 22, 2014)

www.ingramcontent.com/pod-product-compliance
Lightning Source LLC
Chambersburg PA
CBHW071737150726
47998CB00005B/1691